YOUR LIBRARY
WHAT'S IN IT FOR YOU?

John Lolley
Tarrant County Junior College
Fort Worth, Texas

in consultation with

Samuel J. Marino, Ph.D.
Texas Woman's University
Denton, Texas

John Wiley & Sons, Inc.

New York · London · Sydney · Toronto

Editors: Judy Wilson and Irene Brownstone
Production Manager: Ken Burke
Copyeditor: Lorna Cunkle
Artist: Linda Jones
Composition and Make-up: Lorna Cunkle

Photographs on pages viii, 4, 48, 80, and 128 from Culver Pictures, Inc., 660 First Avenue, New York, New York.

Excerpts from the Readers' Guide to Periodical Literature (pages 54, 56, and 60), Applied Science and Technology Index (page 65), Business Periodicals Index (page 67), Art Index (page 69), Education Index (page 71), Social Sciences and Humanities Index (page 73), and Book Review Digest (pages 122 and 124) reprinted by permission from H.W. Wilson Company.

Excerpt from The American College Dictionary, copyright 1967, on page 92 reprinted by permission from Random House, Inc.

Excerpt from The 1973 World Almanac on page 97 reprinted by permission from Newspaper Enterprise Association.

Excerpt from volume 30 of Encyclopedia Americana, copyright 1973, on page 95 reprinted by permission from Americana Corporation.

Excerpt from A Manual for Writers of Term Papers, Theses, and Dissertations, Third Edition, copyright 1967, by Kate L. Turabian, on page 102 reprinted by permission from The University of Chicago Press.

Excerpt from The Home Book of Quotations on page 104 reprinted by permission from Dodd, Mead & Company, New York.

Library of Congress Cataloging in Publication Data

Lolley, John.
   Your library: what's in it for you?

   (Wiley self-teaching guides)
    1. Libraries--Handbooks, manuals, etc. I. Title.
(Z710. L64)   028. 7   73-18293
ISBN 0-471-54365-9

Printed in the United States of America
74 75   10 9 8 7 6 5 4 3

DEDICATED TO

Lynnelle
John Jr.
Joseph

I hear, and I forget.

I see, and I remember.

I do, and I understand.

Preface

Your Library—What's in It for You? is an individualized approach to
teaching the fundamentals of library use. It teaches how to locate books
through the library catalog, how to find appropriate articles in the periodical indexes, and how to answer questions using the various types of
reference books. Librarians spend a major part of their time explain-
ing these items. If students can be taught these basics, then they could
tap the true resources of the library and free the library staff from
those duties which seem to require so much attention and time.

Today's "student" may use many different libraries—the college or
university library, the public library, and a host of specialized libraries
such as those in museums or zoos. Since each of these may have a different system of classifying books and resources within them, my book
discusses both the Dewey Decimal and the Library of Congress systems,
but allows the reader to bypass whatever doesn't apply to his needs.
Within these pages the reader is given a guided tour of a library; he
learns about the services he can expect (such as interlibrary loans,
availability of copiers, and sometimes even typing rooms).

Because the book is self-paced, students are not placed in a situa-
tion of "dead-heat" competition between slow and fast learners in the
classroom. The only goal is learning and each student completes only
that portion of the book that is relevant to his individual needs. Because
each chapter is self-contained, the book has total flexibility. Each
chapter has two parts: the informative part which is supported by
exercises and illustrations, and the practical work which allows the
student to demonstrate his ability and mastery of behavioral objectives.
I have found most library orientation books dull, stiff, and often pedantic. This guide has a light, humorous approach and is presented as if
it were answering actual questions. The student can interact with its
easy, readable format. Once the book is completed, the extensive
index makes it a handy reference work. Pages have been exactly reproduced from the major indexes and references so that the reader can use
the book outside the library.

The guide could be useful in a variety of courses including English (particularly because the Appendix provides basic guidelines for writing a research paper), and college and library orientation courses (both formal and informal). In addition, many libraries are becoming self-help education centers as more adults return to education and training and more community college students commute to their classrooms. This book could be particularly helpful to them. Primarily, I hope it will give all readers access to new publications, skills, and resources they may never have had before.

I would like to thank the many people at Tarrant County Junior College who helped me with this book including the library staff, the counselors, and the more than 3000 students who used the prototype of the book. Special thanks goes to Ralph Man, circulation librarian at TCJC and Judy Wilson, editor of the Wiley Self-Teaching Guides, for her patience and understanding.

Fort Worth, Texas   John L. Lolley
February 1974

Contents

"Welcome to college—and now on to your library orientation."

INTRODUCTION
Why Should I Use This Guide?

"The library is a wonderful place to visit but I certainly wouldn't want to live there!"

True, you may not want to live there but it is very likely that at some time during your academic career you will want to use the materials found in a library. You will need books and periodicals, as well as other resources, to answer assignments, for research and term papers, or simply to read for pleasure. If you are like most people, there are some things you do well and some things you do poorly. So it is with using the library. There are students who find the library a truly wonderful place to visit and to use. To others it is like trying to climb a mountain with a broken leg.

Let me illustrate. A few years ago a man burst into the librarian's office angrily shouting that this library didn't have "a thing in it," and that he was going to quit school. He had waited over eighteen years to come to college after graduating from high school and now after a few weeks it was all over. Why? Well, it seems that he had been assigned a paper to do in the library. He wandered through the building for days on end without finding what he needed. That frustrating experience was enough to make him give up eighteen years of wanting a college education. He walked out the front door of the library, and as far as anyone can tell, he never enrolled in the school again!

Upon investigation we found that the elusive information that he searched for was not really that hard to find. Unfortunately, he had not taken the library orientation course and had never learned to use the library. To him the library was a mountain he could never climb.

"I'm convinced," you say. "But that sounds pretty negative!"

Hold on, friend. Let me now tell you of the many students who every day look for and find the materials they need or the ones who ask their librarians for help and promptly receive it. I haven't mentioned the ones whose grades have improved through skillful library use. Nor have I told you of the hours spent by students reading for the sheer pleasure of it. All of these things occur every day in a library.

The question is, "How will you use your library?"

Upon completion of this guide you should be able to locate books through the use of the library catalog, find periodical articles using the periodical indexes, and answer reference questions from representative reference books. You will learn of the many services offered by your library. Finally, the Appendix includes a guide to help you write a research paper.

GREAT! WHAT AM I SUPPOSED TO DO?

This guide is a chance for you to literally do your own thing. It is an individualized, self-paced course allowing you to work when you want to as fast or slow as you feel. Each chapter in this book is complete in itself. You can proceed from chapter to chapter, master one section and go to the next. The guide is divided into five sections: Chapter 1, The Library Catalog; Chapter 2, Periodical Indexes; Chapter 3, Reference Books; Chapter 4, Library Services; and Appendix, Writing a Research Paper.

We have set it up so that you do not have to spend a lot of time in the library. Each section has a short text with exercises. You can read the text and answer the questions—when and where you want to. Then go to the library for the practical work. We suggest that you go through the text of each section thoroughly before doing the practical work.

Be sure that you read the student objectives. They tell you what you can expect to learn from each section. A pre-test is given for the first three sections. It is not a test in that you will not be graded on it. It is a way for you to see what you already know or don't know about each section.

Take the pre-test. If you answer all of the questions correctly you may go directly to the practical work. If you miss some questions start at the beginning of the text. There is also a post-test which shows you what you have learned.

Who are we? Why, we are the friendly librarians who want to help you . . .

USE YOUR LIBRARY

"Hold it boys, he's coming to the good part now!"

CHAPTER ONE
The Library Catalog

STUDENT OBJECTIVES

After reading the text and completing the exercises on the following subjects:

> Identifying the Book
> The Library Classification System
> Call Numbers
> How to Find Books in the Library Catalog
> The Arrangement of Library Catalogs

the student will be able to locate books in the library catalog by author, title, and subject entry.

PRE-TEST

You may not be able to answer any of these questions. Don't worry, that's why you are using this guide.

1. Most books are identified by at least five elements. Name four.

(a) _author_ (c) _publisher_

(b) _title_ (d) _place of publication_

2. Books are arranged in a library according to a classification system which places all books with the same _subject_ together.

3. Most libraries use one of the two most common classification systems in America today. The Library of Congress uses _letters_ to indicate broad subject areas and the Dewey Decimal system uses _numbers_ to indicate broad subject areas.

✓4. In the library classification system each book is assigned a _call number_ .

5. Books can be entered in the library catalog by at least three ways. Name them.

(a) _author_ (c) _title_

(b) _subject_

✓6. The entry that contains the information found on the title page plus additional information about the book is called the _author_ entry. It is also known as the main entry.

✓7. The cross reference in a library catalog which refers you from a subject not used to one that is used is called a " _See_ " reference.

✓8. The cross reference in a library catalog which directs you to a subject that is related to yours is called a " _see also_ " reference.

9. The two most common arrangements for library catalogs are the dictionary and divided catalog. The method of filing the entries in both catalogs is <u>alphabetically word by word</u>

Remember, you are not expected to answer all or any of these questions. Check your answers on page 46 to see how you did. If you answered all the questions correctly, turn to page 42 and begin the practical work. If you missed some, turn the page and begin with Identifying the Book.

IDENTIFYING THE BOOK

When most people think of a library they think of books, but libraries contain much more than books. Think of a library as a store—a storehouse of information. Just as the items in a store come in various forms, so does the information in a library. It can be in print form as in books or periodicals, but it can also be in the form of films, slides, recordings, video and sound tapes, or almost any format. A library display case of American Indian handicraft is a form of information. This guide, however, will concern itself with the printed materials—the books and periodicals.

Let's take a look at the first of them, the book. It's certainly no mysterious thing, is it? Two covers with pages in the middle. It is the identification of the book which can give students trouble, particularly when the book must be identified as the source of information for term or research papers. The author of a book is the person or persons who wrote the book. The title is the name of the book, that which distinguishes it from other books. The author and title are usually on the back (spine) of the book or perhaps on the front cover. Often, though, it is only the author's last name and a "short" title. Since, in research, it is necessary to know the author's full name and the complete title, we must turn to the title page, which is the first important printed page of the book. The illustration below shows a title page.

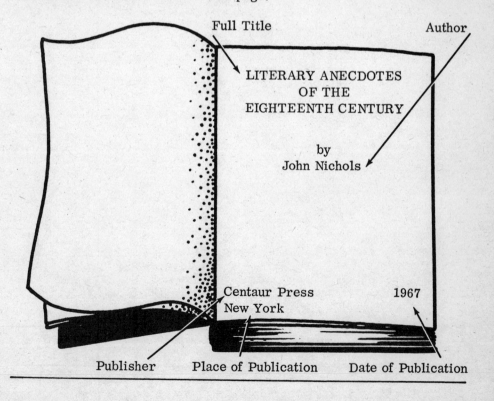

Full Title		Author
LITERARY ANECDOTES OF THE EIGHTEENTH CENTURY		
by John Nichols		
Centaur Press New York		1967
Publisher	Place of Publication	Date of Publication

Notice the complete title, <u>Literary</u> <u>Anecdotes</u> <u>of</u> <u>the</u> <u>Eighteenth</u> <u>Century</u>, followed by the author's full name, John Nichols. Below this is the publisher of the book, Centaur Press, the city where the book was published, New York, and the date when it was published, 1967. This date may also be found on the back of the title page. It is actually the copyright date or the date when the author established his ownership of the book. It would probably be better to use the copyright date when citing the book.

Exercises

1. The person who writes a book is called the ___author___ .

2. The name of the book—that which distinguishes it from other books— is called the ___title___ .

3. The first important printed page, which contains the author, title, publisher, place and date of publication, is called the ___title-page___.

From the illustration below, fill in the blanks.

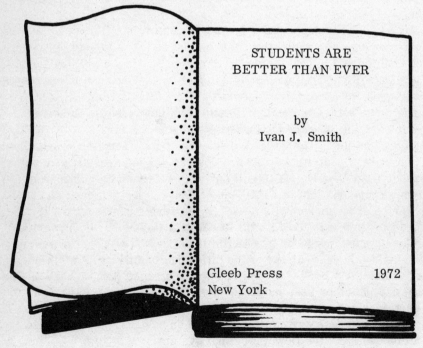

STUDENTS ARE
BETTER THAN EVER

by
Ivan J. Smith

Gleeb Press   1972
New York

4. Author's full name ___Ivan J. Smith___

5. Complete title ___Students Are Better Than Ever___

6. Publisher _____Globe Press_____

7. Place of publication _____New York_____

8. Date of publication _____1972_____

Now check your answers by comparing them with those given on page 46. Easy wasn't it? Moving right along. . .

HOW BOOKS ARE ARRANGED IN A LIBRARY

Wouldn't it be wild if books were arranged in a library by the color of their covers? You could check out some yellow books which might be about horses, some red ones about American history, and maybe some of those pretty pink ones on TV repair.

Don't laugh. It might not be such a bad idea, except that there are a limited number of colors and probably an unlimited number of subjects that books can be about. Most books have at least one thing in common— they do have a subject; that is, they are written to explain or illustrate something. To put it another way, the subject is what the book is about, and you are interested in the subject of the book—not the color of its cover.

Since books for general use are not arranged in a library by the color of their covers or by their size, there must be some logical arrangement which enables you to find them. In libraries books are arranged accord- ing to a classification system. In a classification system, all books on the same subject are placed together.

The two most common classification systems used in American libraries are the Library of Congress classification and the Dewey Deci- mal classification. This guide will discuss both. Find out which classi- fication system your library uses. You can ask any librarian or perhaps a teacher. Another way is to pull any of the circulating books from the shelves or find one that has not been reshelved. On the back there will be a series of numbers and letters. If the series begins with a letter (such as S428. 7) it is the Library of Congress system. If the series begins with numbers (such as 642. 13) it is the Dewey Decimal system. You can already see that one of the differences in the two is that one uses letters to classify books into major subject classes (the Library of Con- gress) and the other uses numbers (the Dewey Decimal). Turn now to the section which covers the classification system for your library. The Library of Congress system is discussed on page 11. Turn to page 17 for a discussion of the Dewey Decimal system.

LIBRARY OF CONGRESS CLASSIFICATION SYSTEM

If your library uses the Library of Congress classification, then it places all of the books on the same subject together under letters of the alphabet. Of the twenty-six letters of the alphabet, twenty-one are used to indicate broad subject areas or classes. These are listed on page 12. Notice that the letter B indicates the broad subject areas philosophy and religion, meaning that all books about philosophy or religion are assigned the letter B. Running down the classification system, we see that H represents the social sciences, with all books about the social sciences assigned the letter H. And so it goes: J is for political science books, K for law books, etc. Now look at the letter N, which is for the fine arts. Notice that the broad subject areas can have subtopics under them. Fine arts has the subtopics NA, for books about architecture, NB for sculpture, and ND for painting, all still under the broad subject area of fine arts.

As you scan the other letters and their subjects, do not try to memorize them unless you feel a compelling desire to do so. You only have to understand that each letter of the alphabet represents a subject of books, and these books are placed together on the library shelf under this letter. The illustration on the following page does not encompass the whole Library of Congress classification—just the twenty-one broad subject areas and some of their subtopics.

Exercises

1. Books are arranged in a library according to a _Classification_ _system_ .

2. In a classification system, all books on the same _subject_ are placed together.

3. The two most common classification systems used by American libraries are _Library of Congress System_ and _Dewey Decimal System_ .

4. The Library of Congress classification uses _letters_ to indicate broad subject areas or classes.

5. Each broad subject area may have _subtopics_ under them, all still within the broad subject area.

Library of Congress Classification System

A General Works

B Philosophy & Religion
  BD Metaphysics
  BF Psychology
  BJ Ethics
  BM Judaism
  BR Christianity

C History (General—
Civilization, Genealogy)

D History—Old World
  DA Great Britain
  DC France
  DE Classical antiquity
  DF Greece
  DK Russia
  DS Asia
  DT Africa

E American History &
General U.S. History

F American History (local)
& Latin American

G Geography, Anthropology,
Folklore, Sports, & Other

H Social Sciences
  HA Statistics
  HB-HD Economics
  HF Commerce
  HG-HJ Finance
  HM Sociology
  HQ Family, marriage,
home
  HV Social pathology

J Political Science

K Law

L Education

M Music

N Fine Arts
  NA Architecture
  NB Sculpture
  ND Painting

P Language & Literature
  PA Classical language &
literature
  PB Celtic language
  PC Romance language
  PD Germanic language
  PE English language
  PN Literary History &
collections
  PQ Romance literature
  PR English literature
  PS American literature
  PT Teutonic literature
  PZ Fiction & Juvenile
literature

Q Science
  QA Mathematics
  QB Astronomy
  QC Physics
  QD Chemistry
  QE Geology
  QH Natural history
  QK Botany
  QL Zoology
  QM Human anatomy
  QP Physiology
  QR Bacteriology

R Medicine
  RD Surgery
  RS Pharmacy
  RT Nursing

S Agriculture, forestry,
animal culture, fish cul-
ture, hunting

T Technology

U Military Science

V Naval Science

Z Bibliography and
library science

6. Using the list on page 12, tell what letters indicate the following broad subject areas or subtopics. (Example: L indicates the subject of education.)

Subject	Library of Congress Letter
(a) Medicine	R
(b) Zoology	QL
(c) Ethics	BJ
(d) Law	K
(e) Nursing	RT
(f) English language	PE
(g) Technology	T

7. The following letters refer to which subjects?

Letter	Subject
(a) HQ	Family, marriage, home
(b) QC	Physics
(c) D	History - Old World
(d) U	Military Science
(e) BF	Psychology
(f) RD	Surgery
(g) M	Music

CALL NUMBERS: LIBRARY OF CONGRESS CLASSIFICATION

"Well, gollygeewhiz, I always wondered how a library arranged all of those books on the shelves. But that still doesn't help me find a particular book out of the thousands in the library."

Surprise, surprise! There is a magical device which allows you to find any book in a library. It's called a call number!

Each book on the shelves is given a call number. The call number identifies a book in much the same manner a social security number identifies a person. Take the social security number 400-52-0979. There may be thousands of people with the same first set of numbers, 400. There may be a smaller number of people with the next set, 52, but only one person has these numbers plus the last numbers, 0979. The same applies to the call number of a book. No two titles have the same call number L901.A53, with L being the letter for the broad subject area education. There may be thousands of other books with the class letter L, but only one will have the remainder of the call number 901.A53.

The call number of a book then consists of the letter (or letters) representing the broad subject area or subtopic the book covers and a series of numbers and letters that further identifies the book. Notice the illustration below; the book has a call number B358.C57. B tells us that the book is on the subject of philosophy or religion. 358.C57 is the unique book number which identifies that particular title.

Call number: B
                       358
                        .C57

B – identifies the broad
       subject area
358 – further identifies the
         subject
C – the first letter of the
       author's last name
57 – a number which further
        identifies the author

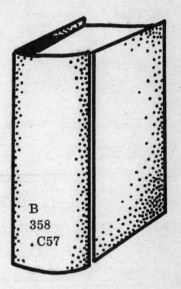

B
358
.C57

After a book receives its call number, it is placed on the shelves first alphabetically by the broad subject area letter(s) and numerically by the subject numbers, then alphabetically and numerically again by the author's letter and number. A book with the call number E421.D3 would be shelved before one with the call number G22.M71. L423.D12 would be shelved before P863.T53, etc. These numbers would be arranged like this:

E	G	L	P	P
421	22	423	863	863
.D3	.M71	.D12	.T53	.W26

The illustration on page 15 shows how the books with these call numbers would look on the shelves.

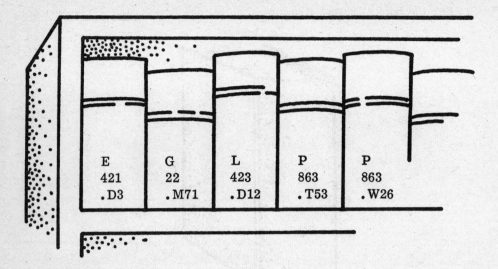

E	G	L	P	P
421	22	423	863	863
.D3	.M71	.D12	.T53	.W26

It should now be apparent that to find any book in the library, you need only know its call number. You then trace it on the shelves alphabetically by the first letter in the call number and numerically by the remaining numbers and letters.

Exercises

1. Each book in the library is assigned a _____call number_____ which is unique to that book and serves in much the same manner as a person's social security number.

2. It consists of a _____letter (s)_____ which identifies the broad subject area of the book and a series of numbers and letters which further identifies the book.

3. For the book illustrated below, the call number is _HQ 21 H43_ .

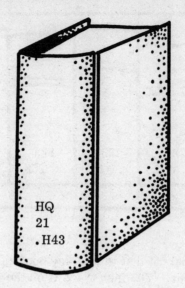

HQ
21
.H43

4. Arrange the call numbers below as they would be found on the shelves.

GG	B	PM	GG	QR	E	GG
770	621	804	721	672	42	70
.C2	.A4	.Z1	.I4	.P925	.C93	.I6

1. B 621 .A4
2. E 42 .C93
3. GG 70 .I6
4. GG 721 .I4
5. GG 770 .C2
6. PM 804 Z1
7 QR 672 .P925

The next few pages discuss

THE DEWEY DECIMAL CLASSIFICATION SYSTEM

If

   I

      were

         you,

I would look them over. There is a good chance that you will want to use
other libraries, particularly the public library, and there are many
libraries which use the Dewey Decimal system.

DEWEY DECIMAL CLASSIFICATION SYSTEM

A library uses a classification system to place together on the shelves books that cover the same subject. Your library may use the Dewey Decimal classification system. The Dewey system divides all knowledge into ten broad subject areas or classes, and assigns numbers to them. These ten classes are listed on page 19. Notice that the number 100 represents all books that cover philosophy, 200 is for books on religion, 300 for those covering the social sciences, and so on. The number 000 is assigned to those books with subjects so general that they cannot fit into the other classes.

Now look at the classification number 500, which represents the pure sciences. Each major class can be subdivided into ten smaller classes or subclasses: 510 is for physics books, etc. Each of the subclasses can also be subdivided into ten smaller classes as in the illustration of the Dewey Decimal number 600 for technology (applied sciences). The number 600 is divided into 610 for medical sciences, 620 for engineering, 630 for agriculture, etc. Notice that 630 is further subdivided into 635, horticulture; 635 is subdivided into 635.9, floriculture; 635.9 subdivides into 635.91, production. It should be apparent that the smallest number (600 in this case) represents the broadest subject area and as the numbers get larger and longer (e.g., 635.91) the subject becomes more specific.

Look over the various broad subject areas or classes and their numbers. It would be nice to be able to remember them. The important thing, however, is to realize that books in the Dewey system are assigned a classification number which identifies the subject. The longer the classification number, the smaller or more specific the subject.

Exercises

1. Books are arranged in a library according to a _classification_ _system_.

2. In a classification system, all books on the same _subject_ are placed together.

3. The two most common classification systems used by American libraries are _Dewey Decimal System_ and _Library of Congress_.

Dewey Decimal Classification System

Dewey Decimal classification broad subject areas or classes:

    000 Generalities
    100 Philosophy and Related Disciplines
    200 Religion
    300 The Social Sciences
    400 Language
    500 Pure Sciences
    600 Technology (Applied Sciences)
    700 The Arts
    800 Literature and Rhetoric
    900 General Geography and History, etc.

Each class can be subdivided into smaller classes or subclasses:

    500 Pure Sciences
        510 Mathematics
        520 Astronomy
        530 Physics
        540 Chemistry
        550 Earth Sciences
        560 Paleontology
        570 Anthropology
        580 Botanical Sciences
        590 Zoological Sciences

The subclasses can be further subdivided into smaller subclasses:

    600 Technology
        610 Medical Sciences
        620 Engineering
        630 Agriculture
            635   Horticulture
            635.9   Floriculture
            635.91   Production

4. The Dewey Decimal classification divides all knowledge into broad
    subject areas or main classes and assigns __numbers__ to
    them.

5. Each main class may be subdivided into __subclasses__,
    which in turn may be further subdivided.

6. Using the information on page 21 tell what numbers indicate the fol-
    lowing main classes or subclasses. (Example: 200 indicates the
    main class Religion.)

Class	Dewey Decimal Number
(a) Psychology	150
(b) Law	340
(c) Music	780
(d) Education	370
(e) Earth Sciences	550
(f) Language	400
(g) Medical Sciences	610

7. The following numbers refer to which classes?

Number	Class
(a) 020	Library Science
(b) 910	General geography
(c) 720	architecture
(d) 330	Economics
(e) 530	Physics
(f) 800	Literature & rhetoric
(g) 690	Buildings

Dewey Decimal Classifications (Second Summary—The 100 Divisions)

000 Generalities
010 Bibliographies & catalogs
020 Library science
030 General encyclopedic works
040 General essays
050 General periodicals
060 General organizations
070 Newspapers & journalism
080 General collections
090 Manuscripts & book rarities

100 Philosophy & related
110 Ontology & methodology
120 Knowledge, cause, purpose, man
130 Pseudo- & parapsychology
140 Specific philosophic viewpoints
150 Psychology
160 Logic
170 Ethics (Moral philosophy)
180 Ancient, med., Oriental philos.
190 Modern Western philosophy

200 Religion
210 Natural religion
220 Bible
230 Christian doctrinal theology
240 Christ. moral & devotional theol.
250 Christ. pastoral, parochial, etc.
260 Christ. social & eccles. theol.
270 Hist. & geog. of Chr. church
280 Christ. denominations & sects
290 Other religions & compar. rel.

300 The social sciences
310 Statistical method & statistics
320 Political science
330 Economics
340 Law
350 Public administration
360 Welfare & association
370 Education
380 Commerce
390 Customs & folklore

400 Language
410 Linguistics & nonverbal lang.
420 English & Anglo-Saxon
430 Germanic languages
440 French, Provencal, Catalan
450 Italian, Romanian, etc.
460 Spanish & Portuguese
470 Italic languages
480 Classical & Greek
490 Other languages

500 Pure sciences
510 Mathematics
520 Astronomy & allied sciences
530 Physics
540 Chemistry & allied sciences
550 Earth sciences
560 Paleontology
570 Anthropolog. & biol. sciences
580 Botanical sciences
590 Zoological sciences

600 Technology (Applied sciences)
610 Medical sciences
620 Engineering & allied operations
630 Agriculture & agric. industries
640 Domestic arts & sciences
650 Business & related enterprises
660 Chemical technology, etc.
670 Manufactures processible
680 Assembled & final products
690 Buildings

700 The arts
710 Civic & landscape art
720 Architecture
730 Sculpture & the plastic arts
740 Drawing & decorative arts
750 Painting & paintings
760 Graphic arts
770 Photography & photographs
780 Music
790 Recreation (recreational arts)

800 Literature & rhetoric
810 American literature in English
820 Engl. & anglo-Saxon literature
830 Germanic languages literature
840 French, Provencal, Catalan lit.
850 Italian, Romanian etc. literature
860 Spanish & Portuguese literature
870 Italic languages literature
880 Classical & Greek literature
890 Lits. of other languages

900 General geog. & history, etc.
910 General geography
920 General biog., geneal., etc.
930 Gen. hist. of ancient world
940 Gen. hist. of modern Europe
950 Gen. hist. of modern Asia
960 Gen. hist. of modern Africa
970 Gen. hist. of North America
980 Gen. hist. of South America
990 Gen. hist. of rest of world

DEWEY DECIMAL CLASSIFICATION: CALL NUMBERS

Now that you have learned one of the great secrets of the Western World —how the library arranges its books on the shelves—there will be no stopping you. The library today, the world tomorrow! You still must learn to find the individual books though. Perhaps the world had better wait.

Since each book is unique it is given a unique number, a call number. The call number identifies a book in much the same manner that a social security number identifies a person. In the social security number 400- 52-0979, there may be thousands of people with the same first set of numbers, 400. There will be a smaller number of people with these numbers along with the next set, 52, but only one person has these numbers plus the last numbers, 0979. The same applies to the call number of a book: no two titles have the same call number. For example, a book entitled Business Information Processing Systems in one library is assigned the call number 635.05E58b. There may be thousands of books with the Dewey Decimal number 635.05, but only one with the remainder of the call number, E58b. Notice in the illustration below that the call number consists of the Dewey Decimal classification number 635.05 and a book number E58b. The call number then consists of a number which indicates the subject and a series of letters and numbers which further identify each book.

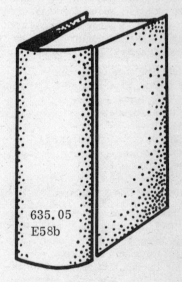

Call number: 635.05
                E58b

635.05 – identifies the subject area
          or class of the book
    E – the first letter in the
        author's last name
  58 – further identifies the
      author
   b – the first letter in the
      first word of the title
      which is not "a," "an,"
      or "the"

635.05
E58b

After a book receives its call number, it is placed on the shelves numerically by numbers in the call number and alphabetically by the letters in the call number. A book with the call number 227.09B75g would be shelved before one with 342.71C39e, 421.1D978r would be before 612W51s, etc. These numbers would be arranged like this:

| 227.09 | 342.71 | 421.1 | 612 | 612.09 |
| B75g | C39e | D978r | W51s | J26s |

The books with these call numbers would look like this on the shelves:

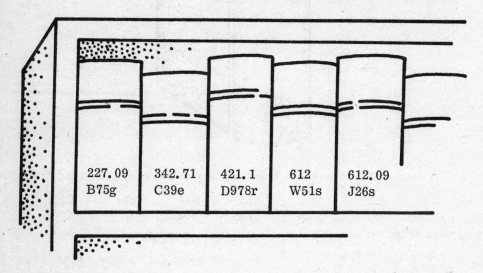

| 227.09 | 342.71 | 421.1 | 612 | 612.09 |
| B75g | C39e | D978r | W51s | J26s |

It should now be apparent that to find any book in the library you need only know its call number. You then trace it on the shelves numerically by the first number in the call number and alphabetically by the remaining letters and numbers.

Exercises

1. Each book in the library is assigned a ___call number___ which is unique to that book and serves in much the same manner as a person's social security number.

2. It consists of a ___number___ which identifies the broad subject of the book and a series of letters and numbers which further identifies the book.

3. For the book illustrated below the call number is *232 B76t*

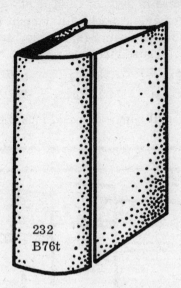

232
B76t

4. Arrange the call numbers below as they would be found on the shelf.

770	621	804	721	672	804	042
C23d	A41j	Z12b	I46c	P925m	L17t	C93t

1. 042 C93t   7. 804 Z12b
2. 621 A41j
3. 672 P925m
4. 721 I46c
5. 770 C23d
6. 804 L17t

Be sure to check your answers before you go on. The correct answers
are given on page 47.

You have now finished the discussion of the Dewey Decimal classification system. Pages 11 through 16 cover the Library of Congress classification system.

If

    I

       were

          you,

I would look them over. There is a good chance that you will want to use other libraries, and many libraries use the Library of Congress classification system.

HOW TO FIND MATERIALS IN THE LIBRARY CATALOG

Remember we suggested that you think of a library as a storehouse of information? Let's pursue that thought further. When you wish to buy something from any large store (one such as Sears or Montgomery Ward) there are several ways to go about it. One way is to browse around looking for the item until you find it. This may take a lot of your time, but then it's kind of fun to look around. Another faster way is to look in the store's catalog where you will find the price, size, color, and other essential facts about each item listed. In other words, the store catalog tells you what the store has to offer and gives a description of each item. Another example might be the catalog for a typical auto parts store. For most people, the catalog is the best way to tell what parts and accessories are available.

Libraries have catalogs, too; they have almost the same function as a store catalog. Again, you can find things in a library the same way as in the store. You can leisurely browse around looking for the books you need. Maybe you'll find them, but maybe you won't. While it may also be kind of fun to browse around, very often you do not have a great amount of time to spare. Here is where the library catalog helps you. It tells you what materials the library has and describes each one. The library catalog becomes even more important with libraries that have closed stacks (i.e., where students are not allowed to go directly to the books). Even where the stacks are open and may be used by anyone, the library catalog offers the best approach. It is true the browser sees all of the books on the same subject shelved together. They represent, however, only the books that have not been checked out. He misses those that are checked out, those waiting to be reshelved, or perhaps those on reserve.

Library catalogs come in several forms. There are book catalogs produced from computer printouts. The catalog may be in microform (either as microfilm or microfiche). The most common form, though, is the card catalog; the information is printed or typed on 3" x 5" cards which are filed alphabetically in trays in a central cabinet.

Regardless of its form, all library catalogs have one thing in common—materials may be located in them by knowing the author, the title, or the subject. In a card catalog, then, there can be one card for the author (the author entry), one card for the title (the title entry), and at least one card for the subject (the subject entry)—all for the same book. Literary works are often an exception; they are not entered in the library catalog under their subjects.

AUTHOR OR MAIN ENTRY IN THE LIBRARY CATALOG

The title page of a book and the author or main entry card for that book from the library catalog are reproduced on pages 28 and 29. Notice that the author entry has all of the information found on the title page: the author's complete name, the joint or co-author's name, the full title, the publisher, and the place of publication. The date of publication for this book is added at the bottom of the page; it actually appears on the copyright page.

You can see that finding the author entry in the library catalog is really like seeing the title page of the book. But that's not all the author entry does for you. It is also called the main entry because it describes other elements of the book, such as how many pages it has and whether it is part of a series of books. Finally it tells you that this book has subject entries in the library catalog, a joint-author entry, and a title entry.

"Say, that's like having a friend at the factory! Without ever seeing the book I know who wrote it, the complete title, when it was written, how long it is, and what it's about."

Study the author or main title entry carefully. You won't be sorry.

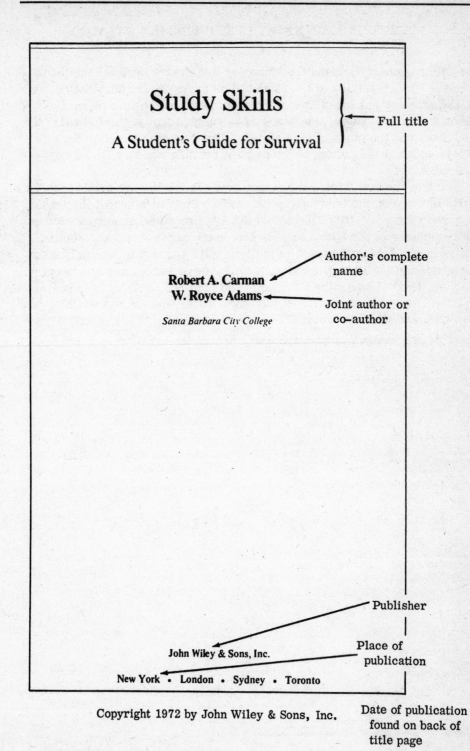

Study Skills

A Student's Guide for Survival

Full title

Robert A. Carman
W. Royce Adams

Santa Barbara City College

Author's complete name

Joint author or co-author

John Wiley & Sons, Inc.

New York • London • Sydney • Toronto

Publisher

Place of publication

Copyright 1972 by John Wiley & Sons, Inc.

Date of publication found on back of title page

Author or Main Entry

```
371.3
C211s    Carman, Robert A
             Study skills; a student's guide for survival
         [by] Robert A. Carman [and] W. Royce Adams.    New
         York, Wiley [1972]
             xi, 256 p.    26 cm.    (Wiley self-teaching
         guides)

             1. Study, Method of - Programmed instruction
         2. Report writing - Programmed instruction   I.
         Adams, W. Royce, joint author   II. Title
                                    Title Entry
```

Call number of this book: Dewey Decimal, 371.3C211s; Library of Congress, LB2395.C26

Author's complete name: Carman, Robert A. (Notice that the author's name is entered in the catalog by last name first.)

Full title of book: Study Skills, A Student's Guide for Survival

Joint or co-author: Adams, W. Royce

Place of publication: New York

Publisher: Wiley

Date of publication: 1972 (The brackets around this date indicate that it was not found on the title page.)

Description of book: 256 pages and 26 centimeters high (There can be other descriptive notes such as maps, illustrations, tables, plates, etc.)

The series note: This book is part of the series Wiley Self-Teaching Guides.

The subject tracings: Study, Method of - Programmed instruction; Report writing - Programmed instruction (These tell the subject of the book and indicate the subject entries in the library catalog.)

Joint or co-author note: Adams, W. Royce

The word "title" means that there is a title entry for this book in the library catalog.

"Man, this seems like a long way to go just to find a book in the library catalog under the author entry!"

Exercises

After you have looked over the main entry, try this little exercise. Since the library catalog tells it all, it's important that you learn the items contained in the main entry. The main entry is used as the basis for most of the other entries. Learn one and you learn them all. Clever people, these librarians. Don't you agree?

```
HE
5623.    McGill, John P
M24         Aim for a job in the trucking industry, by
         John P. McGill and W. L. Robinson.  New York,
         R. Rosen Press,  1972
            160 p.  illus.  22 cm.  (Aim high vocational
         series)


            1. Transportation, Automotive - Vocational
         guidance  2. Transportation, Automotive - United
         States  I. Robinson, William Louis, 1904-
         joint author  II. Title
```

---

1. Call number _HE 5623. M24_
2. Author of book _McGill, John P_
3. Title of book _Aim for a job on the Trucking Industry_
4. Place of publication _New York_
5. Publisher _R. Rosen Press_
6. Date of publication _1972_
7. Number of pages _160_
8. Series note _22 cm. - Aim high vocational series_
9. Subject tracings _Transportation, Automotive etc._
10. Joint author _W. L. Robinson_

Be sure to check your answers before you continue.

TITLE ENTRY IN THE LIBRARY CATALOG

In addition to the author or main entry, a book may be found in the library catalog under its title as a title entry. The title entry is really the author entry with the title typed above it. This is done so that you can receive all of the information about a book when you only know the title. Title entries are filed alphabetically in the library catalog by the first word in the title which is not "a," "an," or "the."

```
                Study skills.
    371.3
    C211s   Carman, Robert A
                Study skills; a student's guide for survival
            [by] Robert A. Carman [and] W. Royce Adams.   New
            York, Wiley [1972]
                xi, 256 p.   26 cm.   (Wiley self-teaching
            guides)


                1. Study, Method of - Programmed instruction
            2. Report writing - Programmed instruction  I.
            Adams, W. Royce, joint author  II. Title
```

"I can't believe it! Three weeks ago I was a plumber.
Then I looked in the library catalog under the title entry
for the book <u>Bullfighting</u> <u>Made</u> <u>Easy</u>. Wish I had looked
up something else . . ."

SUBJECT ENTRY IN THE LIBRARY CATALOG

So there you have it. The book you are looking for may be found by knowing either the author or title. Very often, though, you won't know any
authors or titles for the subject of a given assignment. Rather than rac-
ing to the library and frantically searching among the stacks like a crazy
octopus, you look in the library catalog under your subject for a subject
entry. The subject entry is the author or main entry with the subject
(subject tracing) of the book typed at the top of the card.

A subject entry in the library catalog is illustrated below. In a card
catalog the subject is typed in red at the top of the author or main entry
card. Some libraries prefer to type it in all black capital letters.

```
             REPORT WRITING - PROGRAMMED INSTRUCTION
  371.3
  C211s    Carman, Robert A
              Study skills; a student's guide for survival
           [by] Robert A. Carman [and] W. Royce Adams.   New
           York, Wiley [1972]
              xi, 256 p.    (Wiley self-teaching guides)


              1. Study, Method of - Programmed instruction
           2. Report writing - Programmed instruction  I.
           Adams, W. Royce, joint author  II. Title
```

Subject entries are filed in the library catalog alphabetically by the
first word in the entry. When you look up a subject and find the call
number of a book, do not be completely disappointed if the book is
checked out. Remember that the benefit of a classification system is
that all books on the same subject are shelved together so there will
be other books on your subject. Many students in fact use the subject
entry to find the call number of a book on their subject. They then use
this call number to direct them to the rest of the books that also cover
their subject.

"Clyde, why don't you simply tell them that if they don't
know any authors or titles to look under the subject entry
in the library catalog."

Well, that's about it. You now know the basics for using the library
catalog. There are, however, some other entries which will help you
make even better use of it. Let's look at some of them:

- JOINT-AUTHOR ENTRY: This entry is for a joint or co-
  author and it consists of that author's name typed above the
  author or main entry, last name first.

- CORPORATE ENTRY: A government institution, society,
  corporation, or association may be considered the author
  of a publication prepared for it or by it. (Examples are
  U.S. Department of Commerce, Yale University, American Library Association.)

- PERIODICAL ENTRY: Periodicals are entered in the library catalog under their title. They are filed alphabetically by the first word in the title excluding the articles
  "a," "an," and "the."

- ANALYTIC ENTRY: Often libraries will "analyze" a book
  of short stories, plays, essays, or even chapters that are
  by different authors. This is a good thing because if you
  located a book entitled Great Short Stories you would not
  know which short stories were in the book until you found
  it on the shelves. When the library "analyzes" a book it
  also makes a title entry for each short story or play contained in the book.

WITH A LITTLE HELP FROM YOUR FRIENDS

Alas, there will come a time when you are looking up a subject, say "cars," and you will not find any subject entries in the library catalog. Do we leave you out of gas? We do not! We have prepared cross-reference entries which refer you from a subject not used to one that is used. Your cross reference would look like this:

> CARS (Automobiles)
> see
> AUTOMOBILES

This may also be called a "see" cross reference. See?

"That's nice, but what if I want books on a subject that is somehow connected to the one I am using?"

Again we have your best interest at heart. The library catalog will have "see also" cross references which direct you to a subject that is similar or related to yours.

> AUTOMOBILES
> see also
> COMMERCIAL VEHICLES
> SPORTS CARS
> AUTOMOBILE ENGINEERING
> MOTOR BUSES

"I'll try one more. What if an author doesn't use his real name, say like Samuel Langhorne Clemens writing under the name of Mark Twain?"

Fear not. The library catalog has author cross-reference entries. Yours would look like this.

> Twain, Mark
> see
> Clemens, Samuel Langhorne

Exercises

How about an exercise to check and see if you really can get a little help from your friends. Just write the correct term next to its definition.

author entry
title entry
subject entry
joint–author entry
corporate entry

analytical entry
"see" cross reference
"see also" cross reference
author cross reference
periodical entry

joint-author entry   1. The author or main entry with the joint or co-author's name typed above the entry.

subject entry   2. The author or main entry with the subject of the book typed above the entry.

author cross reference   3. A cross reference which refers you from a false name to the author's real name.

periodical entry   4. The entry which lists periodicals by their titles.

analytical entry   5. The entry that results from an "analysis" of a book of plays, short stories, essays, etc.

author entry   6. The main entry of the library catalog, entered by the author's last name, which contains the information on the title page plus descriptive elements.

"see" cross reference   7. A cross-reference entry which refers you from a subject entry not used in the catalog to one that is used.

title entry   8. The author or main entry plus the title of the book typed above the entry.

"see also" cross reference   9. A cross reference which refers you to other subject entries related to the one you are using.

corporate entry   10. The type of entry used when a government, institution, society, or corporation issues a book.

Check your answers on page 47.

Take a break!

THE ARRANGEMENT OF LIBRARY CATALOGS: CARD CATALOGS

Library catalogs not only come in different forms—book catalog, card catalog, and microform. They may also be arranged differently. The most common type of arrangement is the dictionary catalog, where all of the entries are filed in one alphabetical sequence. The divided catalog literally divides the catalog with the subject entries in one section and author and title entries in another. Many book and microform catalogs will have separate sections for author, title, and subject entries.

All of the arrangements still have this in common: regardless of how the library catalog is arranged, whether in one large catalog or divided into sections, the entries are filed in alphabetical sequence. This brings up the matter of filing thousands and thousands of entries. Filing rules may vary in the different libraries, but here are some generally accepted rules:

1. All entries are arranged alphabetically according to the English alphabet.

2. The entries are arranged in the library catalog word by word. Each word in the entry is considered separately.

Notice how the four sample cards on the next page are arranged. Thomas, John is an author entry, Tomorrow Can Wait is a title entry, TORNADOES is a subject entry, and The Tower of Strength is another title entry. Thomas comes before Tomorrow because "th" comes before "to." Tomorrow comes before TORNADOES because "tom" comes before "tor," and TORNADOES before Tower because, again, "tor" before "tow." In the last title entry, the article "the" is ignored, as are the other articles "a," "an," and their foreign equivalents.

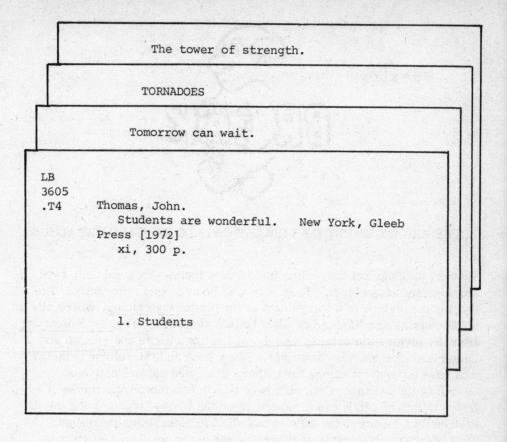

3. Although the article at the beginning of the entry is ignored, articles within the entry are considered in the word-by-word arrangement.

The Tower of Strength: In the title entry "the" is ignored; "tower" is the word that this entry is filed under.

Love Stories of the Turtle: In this title entry, "the" is considered in the word-by-word filing.

4. Abbreviations and numbers are arranged as if they were spelled out. *Spell out numbers!*

For example, "Dr." is filed in the library catalog as if it were "Doctor." "Mr." is filed as if it were "mister." "St." (as in St. Paul) is filed as "Saint." Names beginning with "Mc" or "mac" are usually filed as if they were all "Mac." The number in the title 40 Great Turtles I Have Known is filed in the "f" section of the library catalog as though it were the word "forty."

ARRANGEMENT OF LIBRARY CATALOGS:
BOOK OR MICROFORM CATALOGS

Libraries may arrange the entries in book or microform catalogs in several ways. One method is the dictionary catalog where all of the entries are filed in one alphabetical sequence. The divided catalog literally divides the catalog into a subject section with only subject entries, an author section with author entries, and a title section for title entries. Some libraries have only two sections: a subject section, and author and title section combined. Regardless of how the catalog is arranged, the entries will be filed in an alphabetical sequence.

Many book and microform catalogs are divided catalogs. They are usually produced from a computer printout. This means that the entries must conform to computer characteristics. Notice in the example of a microform catalog on page 40 that all letters are capitalized. In this catalog the place of publication is omitted, along with descriptive notes and subject tracings for the books. The call number comes at the end of the entry. Notice also that this divided catalog is in three sections: author, title, and subject. The entries in each one, as we noted, are filed alphabetically.

AUTHOR CATALOG

*BURROW, JOHN WYON
    EVOLUTION AND SOCIETY. CAMBRIDGE UNIV PRESS 1966
    HM106. B8

*BURROWS, WILLIAM E
    RICHTOFEN: A TRUE HISTORY OF THE RED BARON.
    HARCOURT 1969
    D604. R529

*BURT, SAMUEL M
    INDUSTRY AND VOCATIONAL-TECHNICAL EDUCATION.
    MCGRAW 1967
    LC1045. B8

****

TITLE CATALOG

MONEY AND STOCK PRICES
*SPRINKEL, BERYL
    IRWIN 1962
    HG4539. S58

MONEY GROWS UP IN AMERICAN HISTORY
*BURR, SUSAN S
    SERVICE CENTER FOR T 1962
    HG501. B944

MONEY MEN OF EUROPE
*FERRIS, PAUL
    MACMILLAN 1969
    HG186. A1F47 1969

****

SUBJECT CATALOG

SPORTS

---

*ARMBRUSTER, DAVID ALVIN
    BASIC SKILLS IN SPORTS FOR MEN AND WOMEN. 4TH ED.
    MOSBY 1967
    GV701. A75 1967

*DEWITT, RAYMOND TALMADGE
    TEACHING INDIVIDUAL AND TEAM SPORTS. PRENTICE 1953
    GV701. D4

*KIREILIS, RAMON W
    HANDBOOK OF PHYSICAL ACTIVITIES FOR MEN. DAVIS, F A
    1969
    GV701. K5

POST-TEST

Yes, that's right! The post-test is the same as the pre-test. The pre-test showed you what you already knew or didn't know about the library catalog. The post-test will show what you have learned by comparing the correct answers with those from the pre-test.

1. Most books are identified by at least five elements. Name four.

   (a) _subject_   (c) _Title_

   (b) _author_   (d) _publisher_
   place of publication & date

2. Books are arranged in a library according to a classification system which places all books with the same _subject_ together.

3. Most libraries use one of the two most common classification systems in America today. The Library of Congress uses _letters_ to indicate broad subject areas and the Dewey Decimal system uses _numbers_ to indicate broad subject areas.

4. In the library classification system each book is assigned a " _call number_."

5. Books can be entered in the library catalog by at least three ways. Name them.

   (a) _Title_   (c) _author_

   (b) _Subject_

6. The entry that contains the information found on the title page plus additional information about the book is called the " ~~see also~~ _author_ " entry. It is also known as the main entry.

7. The cross reference in a library catalog which refers you from a subject not used to one that is used is called a " see " ~~see also~~ " " see " reference.

8. The cross reference in a library catalog which directs you to a subject that is related to yours is called a " _see also_ " reference.

9. The two most common arrangements for library catalogs are the dictionary and divided catalog. The method of filing the entries in both catalogs is ___alphabetically "word by word "___

The answers to this post-test are given on page 46.

Sit back, breathe deeply, then relax, because the moment you have been eagerly awaiting is at hand. You are now going to prove to yourself and the entire world that you can locate books in the library catalog and find them in the book stacks.

PRACTICAL WORK

Before you begin:

1. Find out if your library distributes a handbook. Check out the rules and regulations. It won't take much time to read them and you can save a lot of time in the future. The handbook will also tell you the form of the library catalog and the classification system used.

2. Study the floor plan. Locate the library catalog and the stacks. Most high school libraries will have the services and facilities on one floor. Colleges and universities may use several floors. They may also divide the collection by subject with humanities and fine arts on one floor, sciences on another, and so on.

3. Ask for help! If you have any problems, don't get bogged down. Ask for help.

4. As for the exercises, you will be expected to look up a book under each entry and then find it on the shelves. First, write the book information for each entry in the space provided. Then you need to go to the stacks only one time rather than three times. (If your library has closed stacks, fill out the appropriate form for the book and have the book brought to you.)

Author Entries

Using the library catalog, look up <u>any</u> book by at least <u>one</u> of the following authors. Then attempt to find the book on the shelves.

James Baldwin	Charles Darwin	Ernest Hemingway
Margaret Mead	Isaac Asimov	Rachel Carson
John Steinbeck	Arna Bontemps	Mark Twain

Write the book information below: (see back blue cover)

1. Author ___Willa Cather Sibert___
   Title "April Twilights Poems"
   Publisher University of Nebraska Press
   Date of Publication ~~to~~ 1962
   Place of Publication University of Nebraska
   Call number PS 3505 . A87 AB
   I found the book in the stacks. ✓   I did not find the book.____

2. Author _____
   Title _____
   Publisher _____
   Date of Publication _____
   Place of Publication _____
   Call number _____
   I found the book in the stacks.____   I did not find the book.____

Title Entries

Using the library catalog, look up at least <u>one</u> of the following books.
Then attempt to find it on the shelves.

Jonathan Livingston Seagull
Bury My Heart at Wounded Knee
The Making of the President, 1964
Unsafe at Any Speed
2001—a Space Odyssey
Diary of a Young Girl   *See blue sheet*
The Naked Ape
Andersonville
Future Shock
Games People Play

Write the book information below:

Youth and the Bright Medusa

1. Title _____ *Zorba the Greek* _____

   Author _____ *Willa Sibert Cather* _____

   Publisher _____ *Knopf* _____

   Date of Publication _____ *1948* _____

   Place of Publication _____ *Knopf* _____

   Call number _____ *PZ3 . C285YO* _____

   I found the book in the stacks._____ I did not find the book. ✓

2. Title _____ *~~English Poetry~~* —

   Author _____

   Publisher _____

   Date of Publication _____

   Place of publication _____

   Call number _____

   I found the book in the stacks._____ I did not find the book._____

Subject Entries

Using the library catalog, find any book on at least one of the following subjects and attempt to locate it in the stacks. Write the book information in the spaces below. When you go to the stacks, find another book on the same subject and write its book information in the second blank spaces. Be sure to use the "see" cross references if necessary. The subject entries are:

Biology Magazines Business *see blue*
Journalism Nursing Secretaries *sheet*
Boats Sociology Electronics

1. Author *English Poetry* *Walter Blair*
   Title *approaches to Poetry 2nd Ed.*
   Publisher *appleton*
   Date of Publication *1953*
   Place of Publication *appleton 1953*
   Call number *PR 1175 . B634*
   I found the book in the stacks. *✓* I did not find the book. _____

2. Author _____
   Title _____
   Publisher _____
   Date of Publication _____
   Place of Publication _____
   Call number _____

How did you do? Did you find the books you wanted? Answers are not given to practical work because you have many books to choose from and libraries have very different holdings. And remember, if you did not find the book in the stacks, someone may have checked it out. But if you're not sure about the procedure you followed in trying to locate a particular book, ask your librarian.

ANSWERS TO PRE-TEST AND POST-TEST

1. (a) author
   (b) title
   (c) publisher
2. subject
3. letters, numbers
4. call number
5. (a) author
   (b) title
6. author
7. "see"
8. "see also"
9. alphabetically, word by word

(d) place of publication
(e) date of publication

(c) subject

ANSWERS TO EXERCISES

Page 9 ✓

1. author
2. title
3. title page
4. Ivan J. Smith

5. Students Are Better Than Ever
6. Gleeb Press
7. New York
8. 1972

Page 11

1. classification system
2. subject
3. Library of Congress, Dewey Decimal
4. letters
5. subtopics
6. (a) R
   (b) QL
   (c) BJ
   (d) K

   (e) RT
   (f) PE
   (g) T

7. (a) Family, marriage, home
   (b) Physics
   (c) History—Old World
   (d) Military Science

   (e) Psychology
   (f) Surgery
   (g) Music

Page 15

1. call number
2. letter
3. HQ21.H43

4. B621.A4, E42.C93, GG70.I6,
   GG721.I4, GG770.C2, PM804.Z1,
   QR672.P925

Page 18

1. classification system
2. subject
3. Library of Congress, Dewey Decimal
4. numbers
5. subclasses
6. (a) 150   (e) 550
   (b) 340   (f) 400
   (c) 780   (g) 610
   (d) 370
7. (a) Library Science   (e) Physics
   (b) General Geography   (f) Literature and rhetoric
   (c) Architecture   (g) Buildings
   (d) Economics

Page 23

1. call number
2. number
3. 232. B76t

4. 042. C93t, 621. A41j, 672. P925m, 721. I46c, 770. C23d, 804. L17t, 804. Z12b

Page 31

1. HE5623. M24
2. John McGill
3. Aim for a Job in the Trucking Industry
4. New York
5. R. Rosen Press
6. 1972
7. 160
8. Aim high vocational series
9. Transportation, Automotive-vocational guidance
10. William Louis Robinson

Page 36

1. joint-author entry
2. subject entry
3. author cross reference
4. periodical entry
5. analytical entry
6. author entry
7. "see" cross reference
8. title entry
9. "see also" entry
10. corporate entry

"Look at me, Sidney! You've got to tell them
what you know about the <u>Readers' Guide</u>!"

CHAPTER TWO

Periodicals

STUDENT OBJECTIVES

After reading the text and completing the exercises on the following subjects:

> Periodicals in the Library
> The Readers' Guide to Periodical Literature
> Abbreviations of Periodicals Indexed in the Readers' Guide
> The Applied Science and Technology Index
> The Business Periodicals Index
> The Art Index
> The Education Index
> The Social Sciences and Humanities Index

the student will be able to locate articles using the periodical indexes.

PRE–TEST

1. List at least two reasons why you should use periodical articles for
   your library assignmc its, research and term papers, and for general reading.

   (a) _Information is up to date_

   (b) _The information is brief_

2. Periodicals may be in a library in three forms. Name two.

   (a) _Bound_

   (b) _Current_

3. There are two basic types of periodicals, each with a different style
   of writing. Name them.

   (a) Popular periodicals written in a non–scholarly style, often
       heavily illustrated, are called the _General_
       periodical.

   (b) Professional periodicals written by and for members of a pro-
       fession are called _Journal_ .

4. The best way to find periodical articles is to use a library resource
   which lists articles under the subject that they are written about.
   This resource is called a _Reader's Guide_ .
   Periodical Index

5. How does the Readers' Guide to Periodical Literature list the subjects of articles? _alphabetically by the_
   subject

6. The following is a typical entry in the Readers' Guide. Tell what
   each item means.

   Magnificent Apollo. E. K. Gann. Flying. 87:37–56 S '70

   (a) Magnificent Apollo _Title of subject_

   (b) E. K. Gann _author of subject_

   (c) Flying _Subject   Periodical title_

(d) 87 _Volume number_

(e) 37-56 _page number of article_

(f) S '70 _Date_

Check your answers on page 77 to see how you did. If you answered all
the questions correctly, turn to page 76 and begin the practical work.
If you missed some, turn the page and begin with How to Find Periodicals in the Library.

HOW TO FIND PERIODICALS IN THE LIBRARY

A second source in your library storehouse of information is the <u>period-ical</u>, perhaps better known as the magazine. Periodicals differ from books chiefly in that the author of a book discusses his subject in one complete issue or edition whereas periodicals may have an indefinite number of issues and authors. Periodicals usually appear at regular intervals: weekly, monthly, bi-monthly, or quarterly.

You may wonder why you need periodicals if there are books avail-able that cover your subject. One good reason is that <u>there</u> <u>may</u> <u>not</u> <u>be</u> <u>any</u> <u>books</u> <u>that</u> <u>cover</u> <u>your</u> <u>subject</u>! An event or discovery can be so recent that there simply are no books written on it yet. This is parti-cularly true in the scientific fields where research and its results are first described only in periodicals.

It is in the national weeklies such as <u>Time</u>, <u>Newsweek</u>, and <u>U. S.</u> News and World Report that we learn of the everyday political, econom-ic, and social occurrences in the world. Again, these events may be so recent with their full story yet to unfold that there may not have been any books written yet that discuss them.

In addition to being up-to-date, periodical articles are briefer than books and you can often get to the essential facts quicker than in a book.

Periodicals also serve as a mirror of our past. They record the ideas and events of a period in the style and language used at the time. Imagine how much more exciting a periodical account of the San Fran-cisco fire could be than that of a current book which only records it as a historical event.

One very nice thing about periodicals is that no matter what your interest may be, there is probably a periodical published about it. Most periodicals, other than the general and news periodicals, are devoted to a particular subject area. Each issue will have articles written by different authors with varying points of view on the subject.

There are two basic types of periodicals. The first is the <u>general</u> <u>periodical</u>, with articles on many subjects, usually written in a popular style and heavily illustrated. Examples are <u>Sports</u> <u>Illustrated</u>, <u>Ebony</u>, <u>Seventeen</u>, <u>Hot Rod</u>, and <u>Electronics</u> <u>Illustrated</u>.

The second type is the <u>journal</u> or professional periodical with arti-cles that concern a particular profession. Examples are <u>Journal</u> <u>of</u> <u>Home</u> <u>Economics</u>, the <u>Journal</u> <u>of</u> <u>Higher</u> <u>Education</u>, and the <u>Journal</u> <u>of</u> <u>Geology</u>.

Libraries may have periodicals in one or all of the following forms:

1. CURRENT: the most recent issues.
2. BOUND: several issues gathered together and bound in a hard cover.
3. MICROFORM: back issues microphotographed on film or some other medium. (The most common microform for periodicals is microfilm.)

"Say, that's interesting, but how do I find these periodicals?"

The best way is to get the library handbook again. It will tell you the location of the periodical section or periodical room. More than likely it will also locate the bound volumes and microforms. If you don't have a handbook, then ask the librarian.

"O. K., that sounds easy enough. Now that I know where they are, how do I find the articles I want?"

Good question. You can find periodical articles in several ways. The first is the old thumb-and-hope method. You begin by taking the periodicals off the shelves and thumbing through them hoping to find something on your subject. This takes a lot of time, but it does strengthen your thumbs. Unfortunately, you may never find an appropriate article.

The best way to find periodical articles is to use a library resource which lists articles under the subject that they are written about. This resource is called an index, a periodical index. Periodical indexes list articles by their subjects and authors and sometimes by their titles. One of the most useful periodical indexes is the Readers' Guide to Periodical Literature, usually known simply as the Readers' Guide. It indexes articles from general or popular periodicals.

Exercises

1. List at least two reasons why you should use periodical articles for your library assignments, research and term papers, and for general reading.

    (a) _Information is up to date_

    (b) _Information is briefer_

2. Periodicals may be in a library in three forms. They are:

    (a) _Current_ , the most recent issues;

    (b) _Bound_ , several months' issues gathered together and bound in a hard cover;

    (c) _microform_ , back issues microphotographed on film or some other medium.

3. Mark the statement which best describes how you would search for periodical articles.

_____(a) Take off all of the periodicals from the shelves, sit down on the floor, and begin thumbing through them like crazy, hoping to find something somehow.

✓(b) Sit down at the periodical index table, calmly use the periodical indexes while the person who marked the above statement is still sitting on the floor thumbing through the periodicals hoping like crazy he'll find something somehow.

4. The periodical index which lists periodical articles by their subjects, authors, and sometimes their titles is the _periodical_ _index_.

READERS' GUIDE TO PERIODICAL LITERATURE

The Readers' Guide performs much the same function for periodical articles as the library catalog does for books. It is an alphabetical listing of the subjects, authors, and sometimes the titles of periodical articles. Like the library catalog, the entries are filed word-by-word. You will probably use the subject entries much more than the author or title entries. Most of the time you are looking for an appropriate article on your subject and do not know particular authors or titles. The Readers' Guide is published in a small soft-bound issue twice a month September through June and monthly in June and August.

Take a look at the illustration below. It shows some entries from the Readers' Guide. You are going to see many things that you have already learned from using the library catalog.

JUNIOR college teachers. See College professors and instructors
JUNIOR colleges
   Careers and the community colleges: symposium. il Am Educ 8:11-30 Mr '72
   College & careers; what you should know about two-year colleges. G. Keller. il Seventeen 30:160-1 F '71
     See also
   American association of junior colleges
   Brevard junior college, Cocoa, Fla.
   Central Nebraska technical college, Hastings, Neb.
   Kirkwood community college, Cedar Rapids, Ia.
       Federal aid
   Support for two-year colleges. Am Educ 8: 29-30 Mr '72

Notice that the main subject entries are in heavy dark print. The first is "Junior College Teachers." But there is something wrong with this entry, isn't there? The "see" cross reference tells you that this subject entry is not used and it refers you to one that is used. Now look at the next subject entry, "Junior Colleges." Beneath it is an article which concerns the subject of junior colleges.

This then is the arrangement for the Readers' Guide entries. The subject or author entry is in heavy dark print with the articles listed following them and indented for easy reference to separate articles. The title of the article that we are interested in is "College and Careers; What You Should Know about Two-Year Colleges." The title is followed by the name of the author, G. Keller. The letters "il" mean that the article is illustrated. Next comes the title of the periodical, Seventeen. Following the title comes an important series of numbers and letters. The number "30" is the volume number of the periodical, "160-1" indicates the page numbers of the article, and "F '71" is the date of the periodical (February 1971). You can now see how important these numbers and letters are because without them you would have your article but could not locate it!

The next noteworthy item in the illustration which is in dark print is the subtopic, "Federal aid." The subtopic points to articles which are about different aspects of the main subject entry.

Now let's take the Readers' Guide entry apart to be sure you understand what each item is.

Title of article: "Colleges and Careers: What You Should
Know about Two-Year Colleges"

Author of article: G. Keller

Title of periodical: Seventeen

Volume number of periodical: 30

Page numbers of article: 160-161

Date of periodical: February 1971

Did you see the "see also" cross reference? Right, it tells you other subject entries that are related to yours.

EXERCISES

Suppose you are writing a paper on student volunteer work and need a periodical article. Looking in the Readers' Guide you find the following subject entry that looks pertinent:

STUDENT volunteer service. See Volunteer service

You might have first looked under this subject entry:

VOLUNTEER workers. See Volunteer service

Both entries refer you from a subject entry not used to one that is used.

1. What is the correct subject entry? _Volunteer Service_

2. Using the subject entry find an article and fill in the blanks below.

VOLUNTEER farm labor. See Farm labor

VOLUNTEER service
> Three ways to get something done. J. E. Roper. Read Digest 101:39-42+ Ag '72

(a) Title of article _Volunteer farm Labor Service_

(b) Author of article _J. E. Roper_

(c) Title of periodical _Reader's Digest_

(d) Volume number _101_

(e) Page numbers of article _39 - 42_

(f) Date of periodical _August 1972_

ABBREVIATIONS OF PERIODICALS INDEXED
IN THE READERS' GUIDE

In the Readers' Guide entries shown on the previous page and above, the titles of the periodicals were easy to identify. The first was Seventeen. There will be titles, however, that are fairly long and therefore they will be abbreviated. Fortunately at the beginning of each issue of the Readers' Guide, a list of abbreviations of periodicals indexed is there for you to consult. Without this list, who would be able to identify the title of the periodical from the following abbreviation: Am Rec G? (It stands for American Record Guide.) How about UN Mo Chron? This abbreviation is for U. N. Monthly Chronicle. The best way to use this list is to keep one finger on it as you go through the Readers' Guide. When you find an article that has an abbreviation of a title that you can't identify, quickly flip back to the list for the name of the title. The entire list of abbreviations used in the Readers' Guide is given below.

READERS' GUIDE
ABBREVIATIONS OF PERIODICALS INDEXED

ALA Bul—ALA Bulletin
Am Artist—American Artist
Am City—American City
Am For—American Forests
Am Heritage—American Heritage
Am Hist R—American Historical Review
Am Home—American Home
Am Rec G—American Record Guide
America—America
Américas—Américas
Ann Am Acad—Annals of the American Academy of Political and Social Science
Antiques—Antiques
Arch Forum—Architectural Forum
Arch Rec—Architectural Record
Art N—Art News
Atlan—Atlantic
Audubon Mag—Audubon Magazine
Aviation W—Aviation Week and Space Technology
Bet Hom & Gard—Better Homes and Gardens
Bsns W—Business Week
Bul Atomic Sci—Bulletin of the Atomic Scientists
Cath World—Catholic World
Changing T—Changing Times
Christian Cent—Christian Century
Commentary—Commentary
Commonweal—Commonweal
Cong Digest—Congressional Digest
Consumer Bul—Consumer Bulletin
Consumer Rep—Consumer Reports
Craft Horiz—Craft Horizons
Cur Hist—Current History
Dance Mag—Dance Magazine
Dept State Bul—Department of State Bulletin
Design—Design
Duns R—Dun's Review and Modern Industry
Ebony—Ebony
Electr World—Electronics World
Esquire—Esquire
Farm J—Farm Journal (Eastern edition)
Field & S—Field & Stream
Flower Grower—Flower Grower
Flying—Flying
Focus—Focus
For Affairs—Foreign Affairs
Fortune—Fortune
Good H—Good Housekeeping
Harper—Harper's Magazine
Harvard Bsns R—Harvard Business Review
Hi Fi—High Fidelity
Hobbies—Hobbies
Holiday—Holiday
Horizon—Horizon
Horn Bk—Horn Book Magazine
Horticulture—Horticulture
Hot Rod—Hot Rod
House & Gard—House & Garden incorporating Living for Young Homemakers
House B—House Beautiful
Int Concil—International Conciliation
Ladies Home J—Ladies' Home Journal
Library J—Library Journal
Life—Life
Liv Wildn—Living Wilderness
Look—Look (Middle Atlantic edition)
McCalls—McCall's

Miss & Roc—Missiles and Rockets
Mlle—Mademoiselle
Mo Labor R—Monthly Labor Review
Mod Phot—Modern Photography
Motor B—Motor Boating
Motor T—Motor Trend
Mus Am—Musical America
NEA J—NEA Journal
N Y Times Mag—New York Times Magazine
Nat Geog Mag—National Geographic Magazine
Nat Parks Mag—National Parks Magazine
Nat R—National Review (36p issue only, pub. in alternate weeks)
Nation—Nation
Nations Bsns—Nation's Business
Natur Hist—Natural History incorporating Nature Magazine
Negro Hist Bul—Negro History Bulletin
New Repub—New Republic
New Yorker—New Yorker
Newsweek—Newsweek
Opera N—Opera News
Outdoor Life—Outdoor Life
PTA Mag—PTA Magazine
Parents Mag—Parents' Magazine & Better Homemaking
Plays—Plays
Poetry—Poetry
Pop Electr—Popular Electronics
Pop Gard—Popular Gardening
Pop Mech—Popular Mechanics
Pop Phot—Popular Photography
Pop Sci—Popular Science Monthly
Pub W—Publishers' Weekly
Read Digest—Reader's Digest (Great Lakes edition)
Recreation—Recreation
Redbook—Redbook
Reporter—The Reporter
Sat Eve Post—Saturday Evening Post
Sat R—Saturday Review
Sch & Soc—School and Society
Sch Arts—School Arts
Sch Life—School Life
Sci Am—Scientific American
Sci Digest—Science Digest
Sci N L—Science News Letter
Science—Science
Seventeen—Seventeen
Sky & Tel—Sky and Telescope
Sports Illus—Sports Illustrated
Sr Schol—Senior Scholastic (Teacher edition)
Suc Farm—Successful Farming
Sunset—Sunset (Central edition)
Theatre Arts—Theatre Arts
Time—Time
Todays Health—Today's Health
Travel—Travel
U N Rev—United Nations Review
U S Camera—U.S. Camera
U S News—U.S. News & World Report
UNESCO Courier—UNESCO Courier
Vital Speeches—Vital Speeches of the Day
Vogue—Vogue
Wilson Lib Bul—Wilson Library Bulletin
Writer—Writer
Yachting—Yachting
Yale R—Yale Review

EXERCISE

Using "Abbreviations of Periodicals Indexed" on page 57, name the periodicals that the following abbreviations stand for. (For example, Liv Wildn stands for Living Wilderness.)

1. Sci N L _Science News Letter_
2. Mlle _Mademoiselle_
3. Pub W _Publisher's Weekly_
4. Suc Farm _Successful Farming_
5. Am Hist R _American Historical Review_
6. Miss & Roc _Missiles and Rockets_

THERE'S MORE

A valuable extra service of the Readers' Guide is the listing of articles, criticisms, and reviews on movies. Articles may be found under the subject entry, "Moving picture plays." Reviews and criticisms are found under the subtopic "Criticisms, plots, etc." Notice in the illustration on page 59 the subject entry and its articles, the subtopic and its articles, and then the individual movies with the reviews of each one.

The arrangement for movies also applies for articles, criticisms, and reviews of operas and dramas. Under the subject heading "Operas" or "Dramas" you will find the same subtopics—"Criticism, plots, etc." and "Single works"—and the articles that pertain to them.

Subject entry —————→

Subtopic for criticisms, plots, etc. ———→

Reviews of individual movies. (Notice that the movies are listed alphabetically by title.)

Reviews for "The Adventurers" are found in the periodicals listed below it. The first is in America, volume 122, page 426, April 18, 1970.

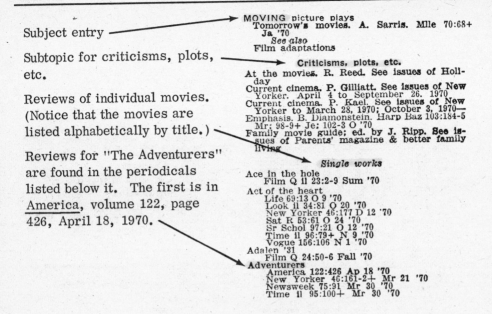

MOVING picture plays
 Tomorrow's movies. A. Sarris. Mlle 70:68+ Ja '70
  See also
 Film adaptations
   Criticisms, plots, etc.
At the movies. R. Reed. See issues of Holliday
Current cinema. P. Gilliatt. See issues of New Yorker. April 4 to September 26. 1970
Current cinema. P. Kael. See issues of New Yorker to March 28, 1970; October 3, 1970— Emphasis. B. Diamonstein. Harp Baz 103:184-5 Mr; 98-9+ Je: 102-3 O '70
Family movie guide; ed. by J. Ripp. See issues of Parents' magazine & better family living
   Single works
Ace in the hole
 Film Q il 23:2-9 Sum '70
Act of the heart
 Life 69:13 O 9 '70
 Look il 34:81 O 20 '70
 New Yorker 46:177 D 12 '70
 Sat R 53:61 O 24 '70
 Sr Schol 97:21 O 12 '70
 Time il 96:79+ N 9 '70
 Vogue 156:106 N 1 '70
Adalen '31
 Film Q 24:50-6 Fall '70
Adventurers
 America 122:426 Ap 18 '70
 New Yorker 46:161-2+ Mr 21 '70
 Newsweek 75:91 Mr 30 '70
 Time il 95:100+ Mr 30 '70

USING THE READERS' GUIDE

And now (at last) a sample page from the Readers' Guide (reproduced on page 60). Notice how the page is divided into two columns. The subject entries are in heavy dark print, arranged alphabetically word-by-word with the articles beneath them. You are soon going to learn about the other periodical indexes. Don't worry, they are all arranged just like the Readers' Guide but are concerned with various subject areas.

READERS' GUIDE TO PERIODICAL LITERATURE

Exercises

1. From the sample page of the <u>Readers' Guide</u> find the first article on the subject "Moving picture festivals." List the information requested below.

   (a) Title of article ___"At the New York movie orgy"___

   (b) Author of article ___C Michener___

   (c) Title of periodical ___Newsweek___

   (d) Volume number of periodical ___80___

   (e) Page number of article ___91___

   (f) Date of periodical ___~~September~~ October 9 1972___

2. Find the first review of the movie "Butterflies Are Free."

   (a) Title of periodical ___America___

   (b) Volume number of periodical ___127: ~~~~___

   (c) Page number of article ___26___

   (d) Date of periodical ___August 5, 1972___

CONGRATULATIONS!

If you found the articles in the <u>Readers' Guide</u> you have learned to use one of the most important resources in a library. Now is the time for the final step in your periodical research. After you have found a good article on your subject you still must determine if the library subscribes to the periodical that the article is in, and if it has the particular issue you want. Most libraries have a current periodical file. It might be in the form of a computer printout or a card file. Some libraries with a card catalog have this information available with the periodical entry. Regardless of how your library lists its periodicals, the periodical card file will contain the information found on the card reproduced on page 62. The periodical card file will be, of course, an alphabetical listing by title.

```
JOURNAL OF GEOGRAPHY    January 1960--

    Microfilm:

        Vol. 59. (Jan. 1960)--Vol. 65 (Dec. 1966).

    Bound:

        Vol. 66 (Jan. 1967)--
```

Title of periodical: Journal of Geography

The date that the library began its subscription to this periodical:
January 1960 (Notice that there is not a date after 1960, meaning
that the library still takes the periodical. A date of January 1960-
1973 would mean that the library stopped taking this periodical the
last issue of 1973.)

You know that the library has current issues of this periodical from the
above statement. The microfilm statement tells you that volume
59 (January 1960) through volume 65 (December 1966) is on microfilm.

The bound statement tells you that beginning with volume 66 (January
1967), the library bound this title.

Now, let's look at that again. This library has the periodical
Journal of Geography in all three forms. It began the subscription in
January 1960. The first six years, from January 1960 to December
1966 are on microfilm. Beginning in January 1967 the library began
binding the periodical. Current issues should be on the current shelves.

Exercise

Your library may not use the type of periodical card file illustrated below. Try to do the exercise anyway. It will help you recognize how a library indicates its periodical holdings. Such a record will show the dates of holdings available and whether current, bound, or on microfilm.

```
ENGLISH JOURNAL    January 1940--

    Microfilm:

        Vol. 29 (Jan. 1940)--Vol. 55 (Dec. 1966).

    Bound:

        Vol. 56 (Jan. 1967)--
```

Using the sample card above, fill in the blanks below.

1. Title of periodical _English Journal_
2. Date library began subscription _January 1940_
3. Microfilm holdings _Vol 29 (Jan 1940) Vol. 55 (Dec. 1966)_
4. Bound volume holdings _Vol. 56 (Jan. 1967)_

APPLIED SCIENCE AND TECHNOLOGY INDEX

One of the nice things about learning how to use the Readers' Guide is that many other major periodical indexes are arranged in the same way except for minor variations. Applied Science and Technology Index, for example, is devoted to periodicals in the scientific and technological fields. It is published monthly (except July). Notice in the illustration on the following page that the subject entries are in heavy dark print with the articles beneath them. The arrangement of the individual articles is identical with that of the Readers' Guide: title of the article, author, title of the periodical, volume number, page numbers, and date of the periodical. The subject entries may also have subtopics where articles deal with some aspect of the subject.

The Applied Science and Technology Index is a subject–entry index (that is, there are no author or title entries). It indexes articles from over 200 periodicals in the fields of aeronautics, automation, chemistry, construction, electricity, engineering, geology, machinery, physics, and transportation. Naturally you don't have to memorize all of these fields. Just remember that for articles of a scientific or technological nature, a good place to look is the Applied Science and Technology Index.

Exercise

From the illustration on the following page, find at least one article about safety laws and regulations, giving the full information about the article. (Some articles will not show an author. These are unsigned articles.)

1. Title of article _Osha in Construction Spells Chaos_
2. Author (if shown) _F. M. Young_
3. Title of periodical (abbreviation only) _Constr. Methods_
4. Volume number _54_
5. Page numbers _77-85_
6. Date of periodical _O_

For this exercise, and others throughout the chapter, you may have chosen a different article. If you're not sure whether your answer is correct, check with a librarian or teacher.

APPLIED SCIENCE & TECHNOLOGY INDEX

BUSINESS PERIODICALS INDEX

The Business Periodicals Index is a subject-entry index to over 170 periodicals in the fields of accounting, advertising, banking and finance, marketing and purchasing, office management, public administration, taxation, and industries and trades.

Again, this index is arranged like the Readers' Guide and the Applied Science and Technology Index. When you look at the illustration on the next page notice the subject entry "Safety laws and regulations." It is the same subject entry as in the Applied Science and Technology Index, isn't it? Both are from the May 1973 issues. The articles are different, however, because one lists articles about safety laws and regulations from a scientific or technological viewpoint and the other lists articles from a business viewpoint.

You can begin to see why you don't have to remember the specific fields each index covers, but only the viewpoint of your paper on the subject. The Business Periodicals Index is published monthly except July.

Exercise

From the illustration of the Business Periodicals Index, find at least one article on the subject of saving.

1. Title of article _Savings ; training for capitalism_
2. Author (if shown) _not shown_
3. Title of periodical _Economist_
4. Volume number _246_
5. Page numbers _92 +_
6. Date of periodical _march 10 , 1973_

BUSINESS PERIODICAL INDEX

RUSSIA—*Continued*

Commercial policy

Possible USSR dumping: panelists urge safeguards. J. Robertson. Electronic N 18:10 Mr 5 '73

Foreign relations
United States

Will Brezhnev help? Economist 246:15-16 F 3 '73

Navy

Another Admiral Fisher? G. Lee. il Economist 246:sup3-4+ Mr 3 '73

SAFES

Bill Randall—securely in Europe [Chubb and son] Scarab. il Director 25:87+ Ja '73

SAFETY advertising

After talks, revisions, ABC airs Allstate air bag spot. Adv Age 44:3 F 5 '73

SAFETY clothing. See Clothing, Protective

SAFETY laws and regulations

AIA to Nixon: OSHA compliance may conflict with environment law [T. L. Jones] Nat Underw (Property ed) 77:1 Ja 19 '73

Avalanche of OSHA mail falls on congressmen; safety called important [J. T. Gillice] Nat Underw (Property ed) 77:26-7 Ja 19 '73

Health and safety costs averaging $170 a man at Budd. R. A. Guiles. Iron Age 211: 25 Ja 25 '73

Health and safety: so who's minding the store? I. Black. Iron Age 211:17 Ja 11 '73

OSHA, big government, and small business. J. R. Nicholas, jr. MSU Bus Topics 21:57-64 Winter '73

OSHA to stress performance standards. A. N. Wecksler. Purchasing 74:23-4+ F 6 '73

Purchasing—OSHA's man in the middle. Purchasing 74:37-49 F 6 '73

See also
Aeronautics—Safety measures—Laws and regulations

SAFETY packaging

Putting the pressure on aerosol safety. il Mod Packaging 46:33-5 F '73

ST LOUIS

Hotels, restaurants, etc.

Personal business [St Louis] Bus W p69-70 Mr 17 '73

SALES

Analysis of legal syntax of standard lease contracts. P. J. Scaletta, jr. and J. L. Walsh. Data Mgt 11:27-33 Ja; 21-2+ F '73

Managers should be briefed on business law [Purchasing] Purchasing 73:35 O 10 '72

National contracting won't meet today's challenges. Purchasing 73:37+ S 19 '72

Put it in writing and then shake hands. J. D. Jackson. Purchasing 74:119+ Ja 23 '73

SALES contests

Dealers seek exotic in incentive trips. R. Smith. Merch W 105:1+ Ja 29 '73

SALES estimates

Mathematical models

System of promotional models. A. G. Rao and G. Lilien. Mgt Sci 19:152-60 O. '72

SALES managers

Supplier execs have the answers. P. Wulff. Purchasing 74:111+ Ja 23 '73

SALES promotion

System of promotional models. A. G. Rao and G. Lilien. Mgt Sci 19:152-60 O '72

Toward a normative model of promotional decision making. D. A. Aaker. bibliog Mgt Sci 19:593-603 F '73

See also
Instruction in use of product

SALESMEN

See also
Purchasing, Industrial—Treatment of salesmen

Salaries, commissions, etc.

Business press salesmen's salaries up, survey finds. Adv Age 44:24 F 5 '73

SALVAGE (waste, etc)

See also
Water reuse

SAMUELSON, Paul A.

Samuelson's text never grows old. por Bus W p58-9 Mr 24 '73

SANCTIONS (international law)

Sanctions against Rhodesia; a report on how a colander works. Economist 246:34+ Mr 3 '73

SANDWICH construction

Honeycomb paperboard debuts in packaging, low-cost reusable paper pallets. panels [Celadyn] il Paperboard Packaging 58:36-8+ F '73

SAN FRANCISCO

See also
Newspapers—San Francisco

Hotels, restaurants, etc.

San Francisco's empty rooms. il Bus W p32 Mr 17 '73

SATELLITES

Saturn moon might support life. Aviation W 98:69 Ja 29 '73

SATELLITES, Artificial

Energy relay satellites urged for shuttle. C. Covault. Aviation W 98:47-8 Ja 8 '73

Astronomical use

Astronomy gains seen in shuttle. C. Covault. Aviation W 98:54-5 Ja 15 '73

Pioneers record solar wind data. Aviation W 98:48-9 Ja 8 '73

Meteorological use

ESSA photographs Soviet forest fires. il Aviation W 98:51-3 Ja 8 '73

Nimbus measures temperatures of earth through cloud cover. Aviation W 98:48 Ja 8 '73

SATURN (planet)

Satellites

See Satellites

SAUDIA ARABIA

See also
Petrochemicals industry—Saudi Arabia

SAVING

1973 forecast of gross national product, consumer spending, saving, and housing. I. Schweiger. J Bus 46:6-10 Ja '73

Savings; training for capitalism. Economist 246:92+ Mr 10 '73

SAVINGS and loan associations

Hottest question in mortgaging: will housing lose its special lenders? S. Wilson. H & Home 43:26 F '73

Advertising

N.Y. bank offers cerebral premiums [N.Y. federal savings & loan assn] Adv Age 44: 63 Ja 15 '73

SAVINGS banks

Remove usury ceilings and other bank reforms. H. W. Albright, jr. Comm & Fin Chr 217:493 F 8 '73

SAWMILLS

Automation

Small log sawmill reflects transition in redwood region [Pacific lumber, Fortuna div] H. Lambert. flow chart il Forest Ind 100: 56-8 F '73

Equipment

Steady upgrading program for chipping headrig operation [Union Camp] R. W. Bryan. il Forest Ind 100:62-3 F '73

SCALES

See also
Weighing

SCALES, Electronic

Pulling the thumb off the scale. il Mod Packaging 46:26-9 F '73

SCHEDULES, School

Application of operations research to school desegregation. R. P. Lutz and others. flow chart Mgt Sci 19 pt2:P 100-P 109 D '72

SCHEDULING (management)

Analytical model of a two-product, one-machine production-inventory system. T. J. Hodgson. bibliog Mgt Sci 19:391-405 D '72

Application of operations research to school desegregation. R. P. Lutz and others. flow chart Mgt Sci 19 pt2:P 100-P 109 D '72

Economic lot size determination in multistage assembly systems. W. B. Crowston and others. bibliog Mgt Sci 19:517-27 Ja '73

Environmental structure and programmed decision effectiveness. R. J. Ebert. bibliog Mgt Sci 19:435-45 D '72

MOS ends work overscheduling, underscheduling. K. W. Bennett. Iron Age 211:32-3 Ja 11 '73

Mathematical programming model for scheduling nursing personnel in a hospital. D. M. Warner and J. Prawda. bibliog Mgt Sci 19:411-22 D '72

Planning and scheduling with visual control systems. il Office 76:45-9 D '72

Short interval scheduling: discipline and results. R. Margiano. Infosystems 20:36+ Ja '73

SCHOOL food service

LA kids get hot meals this summer; their grandparents get something, too. il Inst/Vol Feeding Mgt 72:55-6 Mr 1 '73

SCHOOL management and organization

See also
Schedules, School

SCHOOL schedules. See Schedules, School

SCHOOLS

See also
Public schools

ART INDEX

As you might expect, the Art Index (published four times a year) covers
periodicals in the fields of archaeology, architecture, art history, arts
and crafts, fine arts, interior decoration, photography, and landscape
design. It is arranged like the previous indexes but with some variations.
The articles are indexed by subject and author entries. Artists' exhibi-
tions are indexed under the individual artist. Reproductions of art works
can be located under the name of the artist.

Notice in the illustration on the next page the artist Edvard Erichsen.
A reproduction of his "Little Mermaid" can be found in the periodical
Apollo, volume 96, page 36, August 1972. Now look at the subject
entries in the first column and at the top of the second. They concern
the environment, but as it applies to art (landscaping, architecture,
etc.). You will see in the Education Index similar environment subject
entries, but they will deal with the way this issue applies to education
and educators.

Exercise

1. From the illustration of the Art Index, determine whether there are
   articles under the subject entry "Environmental pollution." If not,
   under what subject entry can they be found?

   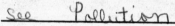 See Pollution

ART INDEX

ENTRANCE fees, Museum. See **Museums and art galleries—Entrance fees**

ENTRANCES and exits
See also
Doors
Doorways
Lich-gates

ENVIRONMENT. See Man—Influence of environment

ENVIRONMENT, Department of. See Great Britain—Department of environment

ENVIRONMENT, School. See School environment

ENVIRONMENT (art)
Adversary spaces. C. Ratcliff. il Artforum 11: 40-4 O '72
Helio Oiticica's propositions. J. Barnitz. il Arts 47:46-8 S '72
Space warps; the work of Gabriele de Vecchi. L. Vergine. il Art & Artists 7:32-5 Ag '72
See also
Conceptual art

ENVIRONMENTAL design
Grant for residential environment study. Design no281:30 My '72
Invisible city. il AD 43 [42]:191 Mr '72
Planners and ecologists. M. Ash. Town & Country Plan 40:219-21 Ap '72; Reply. I. Brown. 40:268 My '72
Self-organizing environments. S. Wellesley-Miller. bibliog diags AD 42:314-16 My '72
Uses and abuses of the planned environment. A. Ravetz. bibliog f il plan tab RIBA J 80 [79]:144-51 Ap '72
See also
School environment

Competitions, awards, etc.
Concorso internazionale di design: la città comeambiente significante. Casabella no365: 76 '72

Congresses, conventions, etc.
Environmental design research association conference, Los Angeles, January 1972. S. Campbell. il AD 42:386-7 Je '72

Exhibitions
Italian design in the '60's: a decade and half. il diags Ind Des 19:54-9 My '72
Italy's super-salesmen come to Moma. il diag Interiors 131:78-83 Jl '72

Research
R&D after the green paper. J. Musgrove. RIBA J 81 [79]:110-11+ Mr '72

ENVIRONMENTAL design education
Proairesis . . . natura e artificio, fattori preferenziali e organicità: che ruolo coprono nel progetto di una nuova università per il design? G. Dorfles. Casabella no365:17-20 '72
See also
Planning education

ENVIRONMENTAL movement
Art and industry; is the artist among those responsible for fragmentation of our environment? D. Dickson. Studio 183:239-40 Je '72; Reply. J. R. H. Yeoman. 184:66 S '72
Best use of volunteers. Country Life 151: 1432 Je 8 '72
In praise of diversity [deficiencies of the psycho-social environment] R. Dubos. AIA J 58:30-3 Jl '72
900 years of concern. B. Dunning. il Country Life 151:1370-2 Je 1 '72

Congresses, conventions, etc.
Earth watch [United Nations conference on environment in Stockholm] Archit Forum 137:89 Jl-Ag '72

ENVIRONMENTAL policy
Battle for the environment, by T. Aldous
Review by P. H. Harvey. Town & Country Plan 40:369-70 Jl '72
Concern for the environment: its impact on construction. G. A. Christie. Archit Rec 151:60 Je '72
Crisis; readings in environmental issues and strategies, ed by R. M. Irving and G. B. Priddle
Review by J. Tivy. Town & Country Plan 40:368 Jl '72
Ecology; theory and practice. RIBA J 80 [79]:47 F '72
Economics and environment, ed by P. Bohm and A. V. Kneese
Review by J. Tivy. Town & Country Plan 40:242-3 Ap '72
From conservation to inaction. P. Self. Town & Country Plan 40:303-4 Je '72
Landmark document. M. O. Urbahn. AIA J 57:16 Ap '72
Only one earth: the care and maintenance of a small planet, by B. Ward and R. Dubos
Review by P. Self. Town & Country Plan 40:367-8 Jl '72
Onward from Stockholm. Country Life 151: 1532 Je 15 '72

President's message. M. O. Urbahn. il AIA J 58:34-6 Jl '72
Regions in distress: a change of heart? C. Ward. Town & Country Plan 40:204-6 Ap '72
State of the environment. Country Life 151: 1368 Je 1 '72

Bibliography
Addresses [Environmental directory] AD 42: 310+ My '72
Book reviews
Only one earth: the care and maintenance of a small planet, by B. Ward and R. Dubos
Review by P. Self. Town & Country Plan 40:367-8 Jl '72

Congresses, conventions, etc.
Environmental balancing act; a report on the UN conference on the environment. C. Amery. Town & Country Plan 40:365-7 Jl '72
Stockholm brief. C. Ward. Town & Country Plan 40:300-2 Je '72
UN Stockholm conference. Roy Town Plan Inst J 58:278 Je '72

ENVIRONMENTAL pollution. See Pollution

ENVIRONMENTAL studies, Centre for. See Centre for environmental studies, London

EPIGRAPHY. See Inscriptions

EPSTEIN, Sir Jacob

Reproductions
Portrait of Linda Christian
Apollo ns 96:[front] 18 O '72
Art N 71:73 O '72

EQUIPMENT, Building. See Building fittings; Mechanical equipment of buildings

EQUIPO Realidad

Reproductions
Birth of Apollo (1972)
Artforum 11:77 O '72

EQUITY association, Artists's. See Artists' equity association

ERASMUS, Desiderius
Second book illuminated by Holbein [Paraphrasis in Evangelium Matthaei in Rijksuniversiteit library in Ghent] I. L. Zupnick. bibliog f il Mast Draw 10 no2:133-7 Summer '72

EREWASH River valley, England
Lawrence's country revisited; the Erewash valley. R. Christian. il Country Life 152: 19-21 Jl 6 '72

ERGONOMICS. See Human engineering

ERICHSEN, Edvard

Reproductions
Little mermaid
Apollo ns 96:[front] 36 S '72

ERICKSON, Steve
Metro state college gallery, Denver; exhibit. R. Lang. Craft Horiz 32:44-5 Ag '72

ERICSSON, Christoffer H.
Sunken Russian frigate. il(incl col cover) diags Archaeology 25:172-9 Je '72

ERMITAZH. See Leningrad—Hermitage

ERNST, Max

Reproductions
La bella stagione (drwg, 1925)
Casabella no365:4 '72
[Disc]
Artforum 10:15 Je '72
Enfants jouant aux astronautes (1969)
Art in Am 60:127 S '72
Art Int 16:23 Summer '72
Figure (1931)
Artforum 11:69 S '72
Les moeurs des feuilles (drwg, 1925)
Burl Mag 114:xxiii Je '72

EROS (Cupid)
Il rilievo di Paride ed Eros [nella Galleria Spada, Roma] R. M. Carra. bibliog f il Boll Arte 43:178-83 O '68

EROTIC art
Other realties; work of John Holmes. H. Wolfram. il(pt col incl cover) Art & Artists 7:24-7 Jl '72
See also
Sex in art

ERTÉ (Romain de Tirtoff)
Erté—a collectors' book for nostalgic connoisseurs. il Connoisseur 181:60-1 S '72

Reproductions
[Print from Signs of man]
Connoisseur 181:[front] 78 S '72
Le reveil des elegances parisiennes (gouache)
Art in Am 60:27 S '72

ERTL, Fritz
Processo agli architetti di Auschwitz. Architettura 17:704-5 Mr '72

ESANATOGLIA master. See Master of Esanatoglia

EDUCATION INDEX

The Education Index (published monthly except July and August) is a subject–entry index to more than 200 periodicals in the field of education. It has the same arrangement as the indexes you have looked at previously.

Notice in the illustration of the Education Index that the subject entries dealing with environment are found in the second column near the top. The articles under these apparently similar entries will differ in their emphasis from those in the Art Index, the Business Periodicals Index, the Applied Science and Technology Index, and the Readers' Guide. The real trick in using the various periodical indexes is to determine what view or emphasis you seek in the articles, and then to select the appropriate index.

Exercise

1. From the illustration of the Education Index, name a subject entry that you might also look under for articles on "Equipment."

   Athletics Equipment

"Let's see now, the school of hard knocks should be in here someplace."

EDUCATION INDEX

SOCIAL SCIENCES AND HUMANITIES INDEX

The Social Sciences and Humanities Index (published four times a year) is an author and title entry index of articles in the fields of anthropology, economics, geography, history, language and literature, philosophy, political science, religion, theology, sociology, and the theatre. You are certainly not expected to memorize all of these fields. In fact, many of them are covered in the other indexes, particularly in the Readers' Guide. The difference between the Social Sciences and Humanities Index and the others is the depth of the articles. The articles listed in this index will come from scholarly or professional journals in these fields. This is not to say that you want to avoid this index. It simply means that if you have need of articles for scholarly research, here is a good place to start. It is an excellent source for articles on authors and their works.

Exercise

From the illustration of the Social Sciences and Humanities Index on page 73, can you find an article about Moby Dick, one of Herman Melville's works? This should be a good exercise for you. Often in your courses, particularly English courses, you must locate articles just like this.

1. Title of article *moby Dick & the Town - Ho's story* *annihilation & ambiguity*
2. Author of article *E. J. Rose*
3. Title of periodical *new England*
4. Volume number *Q 45*
5. Page numbers *541 - 548*
6. Date of periodical *December 1972*

SOCIAL STUDIES AND HUMANITIES INDEX

Exercise

Now that you have studied the various periodical indexes, try the following exercise. It will test your ability to select the best periodical index when searching for articles on a subject. Write the letter standing for the periodical index you would consult in the blank preceding the assignment. The indexes to use and letters designating them are given below.

a. Business Periodicals Index
b. Social Sciences and Humanities Index
c. Applied Science and Technology Index
d. Art Index
e. Education Index
f. Readers' Guide to Periodical Literature

__C__ 1. You are looking for articles on safety standards written from a scientific view.

__D__ 2. Your art teacher asked that you locate a reproduction of a painting by the famous artist Pablo Picasso.

__A__ 3. A friend has suggested that you invest in the stock market. You want an article written by an expert in the field that discusses the market from the business viewpoint.

__F__ 4. One of your favorite singers is Dionne Warwick. Where would you find a popular article about her?

__b__ 5. Your assignment today was to find a scholarly article on a book by Nathaniel Hawthorne.

__E__ 6. In speech class you have to make a presentation on the enrollment in colleges and universities. You need a good article that discusses these statistics.

__F__ 7. Your classmate told you of a fantastic movie but you're not so sure. Where would you locate a review of the movie?

__C__ 8. For physics your research paper deals with the technological advances in pollution control. Where would you locate a scientific article?

__E__ 9. The assignment in Education 401 is to write a paper on the equalization of education. Find an article in one of the periodical indexes.

Check your answers to these questions now. It is important that you learn to select the best periodical index for your subject. As you know, they may have the same subjects, but different viewpoints.

POST-TEST

1. List at least two reasons why you should use periodical articles for your library assignments, research and term papers, and for general reading.

   (a) _The information is recent; up to date_

   (b) _The articles may be newly researched fields that books are not written an._

2. Periodicals may be in a library in three forms. Name two.

   (a) _Bound_

   (b) _current   microform_

3. There are two basic types of periodicals, each with a different style of writing. Name them.

   (a) Popular periodicals written in a non-scholarly style, often heavily illustrated, are called the _general or popular_ periodical.

   (b) Professional periodicals written by and for members of a profession are called _journal_. _or professional_

4. The best way to find periodical articles is to use a library resource which lists articles under the subject that they are written about. This resource is called a _periodical index_.

5. How does the <u>Readers' Guide to Periodical Literature</u> list the subject of articles? _by subject alphabetically._

6. The following is a typical entry in the <u>Readers' Guide</u>. Tell what each item means.

   Magnificent Apollo. E. K. Gann. Flying. 87:37-56 S '70

   (a) Magnificent Apollo _Title of article_

   (b) E. K. Gann _author of article_

   (c) Flying _Periodical title_

(d) 87 _volume number_
(e) 37-56 _page numbers_
(f) S '70 _date of periodical_

Check your answers to this post-test on page 77.

see blue sheet

PRACTICAL WORK

The final part of this section is the practical work with the periodical indexes. You will only be expected to use the Readers' Guide. Remember that all of the other indexes are arranged the same way.

Find any article on at least three of the following subject entries or subtopics in any issue of the Readers' Guide.

Students	Books
Love	College Education
Libraries	Environment

Subject _Sewing_
Title of article _Budget sewing with bandannas_
Author (if shown) _____
Title of periodical _Good Housekeeping_
Volume number _179_
Page numbers _110-111_
Date of periodical _August 1974_

Subject _Dancing_
Title of article _Dancing in the Park_
Author (if shown) _J. Kvasnicka_
Title of periodical _Parks and Recreation_
Volume number _9_
Page numbers _64-65_
Date of periodical _June 74_
_(Je)_

Reader's Guide March 1974 - Feb. 1975

Subject _Travel With Children_

Title of article _How to store your child_

Author (if shown) _R. Joseph_

Title of periodical _Esquire_

Volume number _81_

Page numbers _123 +_

Date of periodical _march 1974_

ANSWERS TO PRE-TEST AND POST-TEST

1. (a) They may contain information not found in books—particularly in the scientific fields.
   (b) The articles will often have the most up-to-date information on a subject too recent for books to be written on it.
   (c) The articles are usually briefer than those found in books, enabling you to get to the essential facts more quickly.
2. (a) current
   (b) bound
   (c) microform
3. (a) general or popular
   (b) journal or professional
4. periodical index
5. alphabetically by subject
6. (a) title of article
   (b) author of article
   (c) periodical title
   (d) volume number
   (e) page number of article
   (f) periodical date

ANSWERS TO EXERCISES

Page 54

1. (a) They may contain information not found in books—particularly in the scientific fields.
   (b) The articles will often have the most up-to-date information on a subject too recent for books to be written about it.
   (c) The articles are usually briefer than those found in books, enabling you to get at the essential facts more quickly.
2. (a) current
   (b) bound
   (c) microform

Page 54 (continued)

3. (a) Aw, come on!
   (b) Right you are!
4. Readers' Guide (There are others too, as we'll see later.)

Page 56

1. Volunteer service
2. (a) "Three Ways to Get Something Done"
   (b) J. E. Roper
   (c) Readers' Digest
   (d) 101
   (e) 39-42
   (f) August 1972

Page 58

1. Science News Letter
2. Mademoiselle
3. Publishers' Weekly
4. Successful Farming
5. American Historical Review
6. Missiles and Rockets

Page 61

1. (a) "At the New York Movie Orgy"
   (b) C. Michener
   (c) Newsweek
   (d) 80
   (e) 91
   (f) October 9, 1972
2. (a) America
   (b) 127
   (c) 76
   (d) August 5, 1972

Page 63

1. English Journal
2. January 1940
3. Volume 29 (January 1940) – Volume 55 (December 1966)
4. Volume 56 (January 1967) – present

Page 64

The first article listed is:
1. "Book on OSHA rules; Do It Anyway"
2. J. M. Beattie
3. Iron Age

Page 64 (continued)

4. 210
5. 17
6. October 19, 1972

Page 66

The first article listed is:
1. "1973 Forecast of Gross National Product, Consumer Spending, Saving and Housing"
2. I. Schweiger
3. J Bus
4. 46
5. 6-10
6. January 1973

Page 68

1. Pollution

Page 70

1. School buildings—Equipment
You might also have chosen either of these:
Athletics—Equipment; Audio-Visual Equipment

Page 72

1. "Annihilation and Ambiguity: Moby Dick and the Town-Ho's Story"
2. E. J. Rose
3. New Engl Q
4. 45
5. 541-58
6. December 1972
You might also have chosen "Zoroastrianism and the Fire Symbolism in Moby Dick."

Page 74

1. c
2. d
3. a
4. f
5. b

6. e
7. f
8. c
9. e

"What? They colored in <u>all</u> of the pictures!"

CHAPTER THREE
Reference Books

STUDENT OBJECTIVES

After reading the text and completing the exercises on the following subjects:

Dictionaries
Encyclopedias
Almanacs
Atlases
Manuals
Handbooks
Yearbooks
Directories
Book Review Digest

the student will be able to answer questions using reference books.

PRE-TEST

✓1. Reference books differ from the regular circulating library books in several ways. Name two.

(a) _They are not read from cover ito cover_

(b) _They do not circulate_

✓2. Reference books come in two distinct classes. Name them.

(a) _general reference books_

(b) _subject reference books_

3. The reference book which gives a broad overview of a subject through brief articles telling the important people, places, and events is called _encyclopedia_.

✓4. The reference book which serves as a guide telling you how to do something is called _manual_.

✓5. The reference book which lists the names and addresses of persons, organizations, or of a particular institution is called

directory.

6. The reference book which presents the events of the immediate past year through brief articles, tables, and charts is called

yearbook.

✓7. A one-volume source for maps, plates, and charts of geographical areas is called _atlas_.

8. The reference book that provides information about words, their spelling, meaning, and punctuation is called _dictionary_.

Check your answers on page 125 to see how you did. If you answered all the questions correctly, turn to page 111 and begin the practical work. If you missed some, turn the page and begin reading about reference books.

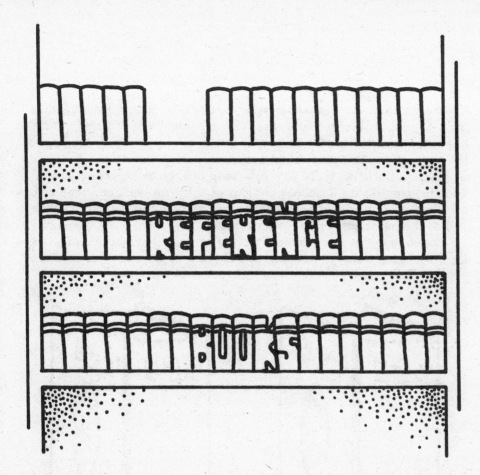

Did you know that in your library storehouse there is an information center? Sure. It's called the reference collection because you "refer" to books in this collection for answers to your questions.

"What kind of questions would I have?"

Well, in a typical day students might want to know, "What was the date of the first Civil Rights Act?" "Who was the 23rd President of the United States?" "I'm writing a paper on John Steinbeck for freshman English and I need a list of his works and their dates." "In biology class the instructor told us to write a brief paragraph on chromosomes." "What is the zip code for Philipsburg, Pennsylvania?" "How do you translate the Spanish word libro?" "Who said, 'If a free society cannot help the many who are poor, it cannot save the few who are rich'?"

Throughout your academic career you will need dates of events, addresses, quotations, formulas, zip codes, spellings, locations of places, names, and lots more. These facts, figures, and fancies must be answered for library assignments and term or research papers.

Naturally you would not want to read an entire book or periodical to find a date, address, or a name. Rather you would prefer some library resource that had such explicit information arranged for quick use and without all of the text usually found in the regular library books. In other words, you want a short cut. There are such resources. They are called reference books.

You can look for specific facts in a reference book without reading from cover to cover to find them. The information is ordinarily entered in a brief, concise form. Reference books also differ from the regular library books in that they do not circulate.

In most libraries there is a reference section or reference room. Look in your library handbook or floor plan for its location. The reference books are easily recognized because right above the call number will be the letter "R" or the letters "REF."

Notice that reference books have the same call numbers as the regular circulating library books and are shelved in the same arrangement.

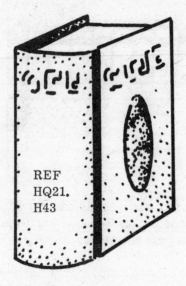

REF
HQ21.
H43

Library of Congress

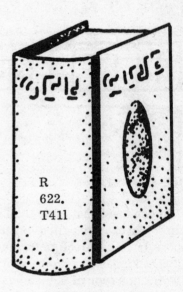

R
622.
T411

Dewey Decimal

DO I HAVE TO REMEMBER ALL OF THEM?

There are reference books on almost every subject in the classification system.

"Do I have to remember all of them?"

Probably at this point you should not be concerned with specific titles of reference books. Rather learn the type of reference book usually found in most subject areas. If you learn the types of reference books that are available, then all you have to do is determine the call number for the broad subject area and you will find all of the books on that subject together.

To find the place where your subject's reference books are, use the library catalog and look under the title entry of a particular reference book. If you don't know any titles, look under the subject entry. Suppose your library uses the Dewey Decimal system and you find a science reference book with the call number R621.T421. You then go to the 600's in the reference section and there will be all of the types of reference books about applied science. The same applies for the book with the Library of Congress call number REF L213.C42. (An even easier way would be to learn the classification letter for education, which is "L." All the reference books about education would be found together in that section.)

Since all the reference books on the same subject are grouped together on the shelves you do not have to memorize a lot of titles. Just remember that most of the subject areas will be covered by the basic types of reference books. Find one and you find them all.

Reference books come in two classes. The first class includes the general reference books: dictionaries, encyclopedias, almanacs, atlases, yearbooks, handbooks, manuals, and directories. These are the basic types of reference books you will learn.

The second class of reference books includes the subject reference books. These are books about one particular subject: the Encyclopedia of Religion, the Dictionary of Geology, Chilton's Auto Repair Manual, or the American Electronics Handbook.

Let's first take a look at the various types of reference books. Study them carefully until you are reasonably sure of the information each contains and how the information is arranged.

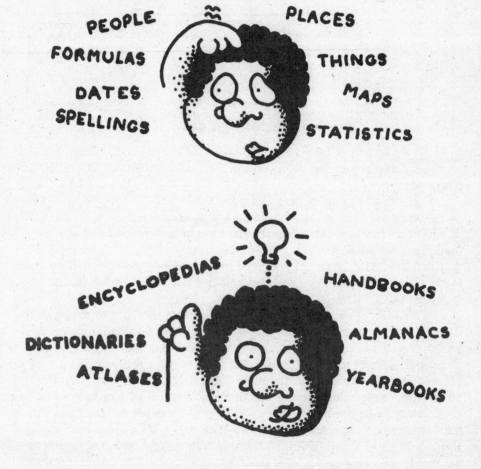

ENCYCLOPEDIAS

General encyclopedias contain information on almost all subjects. They attempt to give a broad overview of a subject, usually through brief articles which describe the subject and tell the dates and people involved. The articles are written by experts in the subject area. Encyclopedias can be one-volume works or multi-volume sets. The subjects are usually arranged alphabetically with an index either at the end of each volume or with a complete index in the last volume of the set.

DICTIONARIES

General dictionaries provide information about words, their spelling, meaning, pronunciation, where they came from, and how they are used. The words are entered alphabetically letter-by-letter.

ALMANACS

The general almanacs give facts, statistics, and basic information on almost everything from agriculture to zoos. They are an excellent reference source for population, business, sports, and agricultural statistics. They also list the elected officials of state and local governments. A typical almanac will include a section of important events that occurred during the year.

ATLASES

An atlas is usually a one-volume source for maps, plates, and charts of geographical areas. Many atlases will have short articles, tables of statistics, or additional maps showing population density, climate, rainfall, vegetation, mineral resources, principal products, or other important information about the area.

YEARBOOKS

A yearbook is literally a book of the year presenting events of the immediate past year through brief articles, tables, and charts. The supplement to an encyclopedia is a yearbook. Many governmental agencies issue yearbooks that cover important national trends and statistics.

HANDBOOKS

A handbook provides broad factual information on a particular subject. It is a "handy" reference source arranged in a brief, easy-to-consult format. One example is the American Electrician's Handbook which employs brief definitions, tables, charts, and illustrations and is an indispensable source for ready reference on electricity.

MANUALS

A manual is similar to a handbook but serves more as a guide. It can give instructions telling you how to do something, as Glenn's Auto Repair Manual does, or it can outline the arrangement of an agency, as U. S. Government Organization Manual does.

DIRECTORIES

A directory is a listing of the names and addresses of the people included in a particular organization or institution. The U. S. Congressional Directory, for example, lists governmental officials and their positions. A directory could also be a listing of the names and addresses of many similar organizations.

You can see that the information provided by each of these types of general reference books is different. In order to make the best use of a reference collection, you should know the amount and kind of reference each type offers. For instance, the title of the book Dictionary of Geological Terms tells you that the book contains terms commonly used in geology, listed alphabetically in a typical dictionary arrangement, with short definitions. Science News Yearbook, on the other hand, will be a review of the scientific events of the year as conveyed by the word "yearbook" in the title. The Encyclopedia of American History would more than likely have brief articles about American history giving a broad overview of each item covered. In other words, the title will often tell you exactly what each reference book offers and how it is arranged.

Exercises

After you have studied the types of reference books carefully, do the following exercise. Do not hesitate to look back if you are unsure of the answers. Write the name of the type of reference book which corresponds best to each definition below.

almanac. *1.* Attempts to give facts, statistics, and basic information on almost everything from agriculture to zoos.

Atlas 2. Usually a one-volume source for maps and supporting information on a geographical area.

Directory 3. Lists the names and addresses of persons, organizations, or institutions.

Manual 4. A guide which tells you how to do something in a specific field.

yearbook 5. A work which presents the immediate past years' events in a particular subject.

Dictionary 6. Contains information about words, their spelling, pronunciation, etc.

Encyclopedia 7. A one-volume or multi-volume work containing information on almost all subjects with brief articles giving an overview of the subject.

handbook *8.* A handy ready-reference source providing broad factual knowledge arranged in a brief, easy-to-consult format.

REFERENCE BOOKS AND THE LIBRARY CATALOG

Before looking at the subject reference books, let's see how reference books are found in the library catalog. You can find nonfiction books in the library catalog generally under the author, title, and subject entries. Remember this because we have based this section of the guide on the premise that you do not have to memorize a lot of authors or titles of reference books. Therefore, you will do best to use the subject entry when looking up reference books in the library catalog. In order to find a reference book on any subject, look under the subject, and then under the subtopic "Dictionaries," "Encyclopedias," or "Handbooks, manuals, etc." A catalog card for a reference book in a library with a Library of Congress classification would look like the one reproduced on the next page.

```
R
GV              SPORTS - DICTIONARIES
567
.S3      Salak, John S
            Dictionary of American sports.  ` New York,
         Philosophical Library [1961]
            xiv, 491 p.    23 cm.




            1. Sports - Dictionaries
```

A microfilmed or book catalog entry on a reference book in a library
with a Library of Congress classification system might look like this:

- -

SPORTS - DICTIONARIES
Pratt, John Lowell
    Official Encyclopedia of Sports. Watts, 1964
    GV567. P59 REFERENCE

- -

DICTIONARIES

You have used dictionaries before so you know that a dictionary will give
the correct spelling of a word, its pronunciation, and its definition.
"When I use a word it means just what I choose it to mean—neither more
nor less," said the great philosopher, Humpty Dumpty. Words, though,
may have several meanings. Do you really need to know all the meanings of a word? Well, most of us, unlike Humpty Dumpty, cannot com-
mand others to understand the meaning that we choose for a word. Besides, you know what happened to him!
    Do you need to know many words? If you like to express yourself,
you do. Like wearing different clothes, we like to use different words
so that we do not appear to be the same all of the time. In other "words,"
the way we talk is one of the many things that make each of us an individual.

You will see that some dictionaries contain much more than just information about words. They will also give information about famous people, important historical events, famous characters in books, and information about countries, states, and cities. Many will have black and white illustrated pictures and full color plates. So a dictionary can be like a mini-library. You really ought to own one.

Dictionaries come in various sizes, not only physically but in the amount of information they give for each word. The one that you will study on the following page is called an abridged dictionary because it does not go into as much detail as an "unabridged" dictionary.

In the illustration of a dictionary on page 92 you will see that the words are entered in heavy black print. They are listed from the top of the page to the bottom, alphabetically. Find the word "gorilla" in the first column. Notice that it is between the words "gorhen" and "Göring," as each letter is considered in a letter-by-letter arrangement. Let's examine each item in the entry.

> go·ril·la (gə ril′ə), <u>n</u>. 1. the largest of the anthropoid apes Gorilla <u>gorilla</u>, ground-living and vegetarian, of western equatorial Africa and the Kivu highlands. 2. an ugly brutal fellow. [t. NL, t. Gk.; said to be of African orig.] —go·ril′la·like′, <u>adj</u>.

The main word entry, "gorilla," is in heavy dark print. This is followed by a section in parentheses showing how the word is pronounced. There will be a letter or letters telling you what part of speech the word is; "n" stands for noun, "adj" for adjective, "adv" for adverb, etc. Finally there is a definition of the word; in this case there are two definitions. After the second definition there is a section in brackets which tells where the word first originated. The last item in the entry is an adjective for the word "gorilla."

Exercise

From the illustration on page 92, find the word "gospel." Tell what part of speech it is and at least two of its meanings.

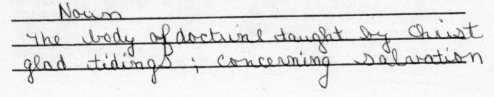

Noun
The body of doctrine taught by Christ
glad tidings; concerning salvation

gore¹ (gōr), *n.* blood that is shed, esp. when clotted. [ME; OE *gor* dung, dirt, c. D *goor*, OHG *gor* filth]

gore² (gōr), *v.t.* gored, goring. (of an animal) to pierce with the horns or tusks. [ME *goren*. Cf. GORE³]

gore³ (gōr), *n., v.,* gored, goring. —*n.* 1. a triangular piece of cloth, etc., inserted in a garment, a sail, etc., to give greater width or secure the desired shape or adjustment. 2. one of the breadths (mostly tapering, or shaped) of a woman's skirt. —*v.t.* 3. to make or furnish with a gore or gores. [ME; OE *gāra* corner (c. G *gehre* gusset), der. *gār* spear] —gored, *adj.* —gor'ing, *n.*

Gor·gas (gôr'gəs), *n.* William Crawford, 1854–1920, surgeon general in the U.S. Army; chief sanitation expert in the building of the Panama Canal.

gorge (gôrj), *n., v.,* gorged, gorging. —*n.* 1. a narrow cleft with steep, rocky walls, esp. one through which a stream runs. 2. a gorging or gluttonous meal. 3. that which is swallowed; contents of the stomach. 4. strong disgust; repulsion: *one's gorge rises in resentment.* 5. a choking mass. 6. *Fort.* the rear entrance or part of a bastion or similar outwork. See diag. under bastion. 7. *Archaic.* the throat; gullet. —*v.t.* 8. to stuff with food (mainly reflexive and passive): *gorged with food, he gorged himself.* 9. to swallow, esp. greedily. 10. to choke up (mainly passive). —*v.i.* 11. to eat greedily. [ME, t. OF: throat, g. LL *gurga,* b. L *gurges* stream, abyss and *gula* throat] —gorg'er, *n.* —Syn. 8. glut, stuff. 9. bolt, gulp, gobble.

gor·geous (gôr'jəs), *adj.* sumptuous; magnificent; splendid in appearance or coloring. [late ME, t. OF: m. *gorgias* fashionable, gay; orig. uncert.] —gor'geous·ly, *adv.* —gor'geous·ness, *n.* —Syn. rich, superb, grand; brilliant, resplendent. See magnificent.

gor·ger·in (gôr'jər ĭn), *n. Archit.* the necklike portion of a capital of a column, or a feature forming the junction between a shaft and its capital. [t. F, der. *gorge* throat]

gor·get (gôr'jĭt), *n.* 1. a piece of armor for the throat. 2. a form of wimple, or neck and chest covering, worn by women in the Middle Ages. 3. a patch on the throat of a bird or other animal, distinguished by its color or otherwise. [late ME, t. OF: m. *gorgète,* dim. of *gorge* throat]

G. Gorget (def. 1). 15th century
A. Attached to the brigandine
B. Worn over mail

Gor·gon (gôr'gən), *n.* 1. *Gk. Legend.* any of three sisters, Stheno, Euryale, and Medusa, whose heads were covered with snakes instead of hair, and whose glance turned the beholder to stone. 2. (*l.c.*) a terrible or repulsive woman. —Gor·go·ni·an (gôr gō'nĭ ən), *adj.*

gor·go·nei·on (gôr'gə nē'ŏn), *n., pl.* -neia (-nē'ə). a representation of the head of a Gorgon, esp. that of Medusa. [t. Gk.]

Gor·gon·zo·la (gôr'gən zō'lə), *n.* a strongly flavored, Italian, semihard variety of milk cheese veined with mold. [named after *Gorgonzola,* town in N Italy]

gor·hen (gôr'hĕn'), *n.* the female red grouse. [cf. GORCOCK]

go·ril·la (gə rĭl'ə), *n.* 1. the largest of the anthropoid apes, *Gorilla gorilla,* ground-living and vegetarian, of western equatorial Africa and the Kivu highlands. 2. an ugly, brutal fellow. [t. NL, t. Gk.; said to be of African orig.] —go·ril'la·like', *adj.*

Gorilla (def. 1). *Gorilla gorilla* (6 ft. high; standing height 5½ ft.)

Gö·ring (gœ'rĭng), *n.* Hermann (hĕr'mǎn), Goering.

Go·ri·zia (gō rē'tsyä), *n.* a city in NE Italy, on the Isonzo river, N of Trieste. 42,000 (est. 1954). German, Görz (gœrts).

Gor·ki (gôr'kĭ), *n.* 1. Maxim (mǎk sēm'), (*Aleksvey Maksimovich Pyeshkov*) 1868–1936, Russian novelist, short-story writer, and dramatist. 2. Formerly, Nizhni Novgorod. a city in the central Soviet Union in Europe, on the Volga. 876,000 (est. 1956).

Gör·litz (gœr'lĭts), *n.* a city in East Germany, on the Neisse river (the Polish boundary). 96,147 (est. 1955).

Gor·lov·ka (gôr lôf'kä), *n.* a city in the SW Soviet Union. 240,000 (est. 1956).

gor·mand (gôr'mənd), *n.* gourmand.

gor·mand·ize (gôr'mən dīz'), *v.,* -ized, -izing, *n.* —*v.i., v.t.* 1. to eat like a glutton. [v. use of n.] —*n.* 2. *Rare.* the habits of a glutton. [t. F: m. *gourmandise* gluttony] —gor'mand·iz'er, *n.*

gorse (gôrs), *n. Chiefly Brit.* furze. [ME *gorst,* OE *gors(t);* akin to G *gerst,* L *hordeum* barley] —gors'y, *adj.*

gor·y (gôr'ĭ), *adj.,* gorier, goriest. 1. covered or stained with gore; bloody. 2. resembling gore. —gor'i·ly, *adv.* —gor'i·ness, *n.*

gosh (gŏsh), *interj.* an exclamation or mild oath. [a euphemistic var. of *God!*]

gos·hawk (gŏs'hôk'), *n.* any of various powerful, short-winged hawks formerly much used

Goshawk. *Accipiter gentilis* (20 to 23 in. long)

in falconry, as *Accipiter gentilis* of Europe and America. [ME *goshauke,* OE *gōshafoc* goosehawk]

Go·shen (gō'shən), *n.* 1. a pastoral region in Lower Egypt, colonized by the Israelites before the Exodus. Gen. 45:10, etc. 2. a land or place of plenty and comfort.

Goshen (def. 1). 1450 B.C.

gos·ling (gŏz'lĭng), *n.* 1. a young goose. 2. a foolish, inexperienced person. [ME *goselyng,* var. (by assoc. with GOOSE) of *geslyng,* t. Scand.; cf. Icel. *gæslingr,* f. *gās* goose + *-lingr,* dim. suffix (see -LING¹)]

gos·pel (gŏs'pəl), *n.* 1. the body of doctrine taught by Christ and the apostles; Christian revelation. 2. glad tidings, esp. concerning salvation and the kingdom of God as announced to the world by Christ. 3. the story of Christ's life and teachings, esp. as contained in the first four books of the New Testament. 4. (*usually cap.*) one of these books. 5. (*often cap.*) *Eccles.* an extract from one of the four Gospels, forming part of the Eucharistic service in certain churches. 6. *Colloq.* something regarded as true and implicitly believed: *to take for gospel.* 7. a doctrine regarded as of prime importance: *political gospel.* —*adj.* 8. pertaining to the gospel. 9. in accordance with the gospel; evangelical. [ME *go(d)spel,* OE *gōdspel,* f. *gōd* GOOD + *spell* tidings (SPELL²), trans. of L *evangelium.* See EVANGEL]

gos·pel·er (gŏs'pəl ər), *n. Eccles.* one who reads or sings the Gospel (def. 5). Also, esp. *Brit.,* gos'pel·ler.

Gos·plan (gŏs plän'), *n. U.S.S.R.* official planning organization, which draws up plans embracing trade and industry, agriculture, education, and popular health. [f. *gos(udar)* national + *plan* PLAN]

gos·sa·mer (gŏs'ə mər), *n.* 1. a fine filmy cobweb, seen on grass and bushes, or floating in the air in calm weather, esp. in autumn. 2. a thread or a web of this substance. 3. an extremely delicate variety of gauze. 4. any thin, light fabric. 5. a thin, waterproof outer garment, esp. for women. —*adj.* 6. Also, gos·sa·mer·y (gŏs'ə mə rĭ). of or like gossamer; thin and light. [ME *gos(e)-somer.* See GOOSE, SUMMER; possibly first used as name for late mild autumn (Indian summer), time when goose was a favorite dish (cf. G *gänsemonat* November), then transferred to the filmy matter also frequent at that time of year]

Gosse (gŏs, gôs), *n.* Sir Edmund William, 1849–1928, British critic and poet.

gos·sip (gŏs'əp), *n., v.,* -siped, -siping. —*n.* 1. idle talk, esp. about the affairs of others. 2. light, familiar talk or writing. 3. a person; esp. a woman, given to tattling or idle talk. 4. *Archaic.* a friend, esp. a woman. 5. *Archaic or Dial.* a godparent. —*v.i.* 6. to talk idly, esp. about the affairs of others; go about tattling. —*v.t.* 7. to repeat like a gossip. 8. *Archaic.* to stand godparent to. [ME *gossib,* OE *godsibb,* orig., godparent, f. *god* GOD + *sibb* related (see SIB¹, adj.] —gos'sip·er, *n.* —gos'sip·ing, *n.* —gos'sip·ing·ly, *adv.* —Syn. 1. GOSSIP, SCANDAL apply to idle talk and newsmongering about the affairs of others. GOSSIP is light chat or talk: *gossip about the neighbors.* SCANDAL is rumor or general talk that is damaging to reputation; it is usually more or less malicious: *a scandal involving bribes.*

gos·sip·mon·ger (gŏs'əp mŭng'gər), *n.* one especially addicted to gossiping.

gos·sip·y (gŏs'ə pĭ), *adj.* 1. given to or fond of gossip. 2. full of gossip.

gos·soon (gŏ sōōn'), *n. Anglo-Irish.* 1. a boy. 2. a male servant. [alter. of GARÇON]

got (gŏt), *v.* pt. and pp. of get.

Go·ta·ma (gō'tə ma, gō'-), *n.* Buddha. See Gautama.

Gö·te·borg (yœ'tə bôr'y), *n.* a seaport in SW Sweden, on the Kattegat. 367,579 (est. 1953). Also, Goth·en·burg (gŏt'ən bûrg').

Goth (gŏth), *n.* 1. one of a Teutonic people who, in the 3rd to 5th century, invaded and settled in parts of the Roman Empire. 2. a barbarian; rude person. [ME *Gothe,* t. LL: m.s. *Gothī,* pl.; r. OE *Gotan,* pl. (*Gota,* sing.), c. Goth. *Gut-* in *Gut-thiuda* Goth people]

Goth., Gothic.

Go·tha (gō'tä), *n.* a city in East Germany, in Thuringia, 57,639 (est. 1955).

Goth·am (gŏth'əm, gō'thəm *for* 1; gŏt'əm *for* 2), *n.* 1. the city of New York. 2. an English village, proverbial for the foolishness of its inhabitants.

Goth·ic (gŏth'ĭk), *adj.* 1. *Archit.* denoting or pertaining to a style originating in France and spreading over western Europe from the 12th to the 16th century, characterized by a design emphasizing skeleton construction, the elimination of wall planes, the comparatively great height of the buildings, the pointed arch, rib vaulting, and the flying buttress. 2. (orig. in derogatory use) denoting all European art of this period. 3. (sometimes in disparagement) pertaining to the Middle Ages; barbarous; rude. 4. (esp. in literature) stressing irregularity and details, usually of a grotesque or horrible nature: *a Gothic novel.* —*n.* 5. Gothic architecture, sculpture, or decoration. 6. an extinct Germanic language, preserved especially in Ulfilas' Bible (4th cent.). 7. *Brit.* black letter. 8. (*l.c.*) *U.S.* a square-cut printing type, without serifs or hairlines. [t. LL: s. *Gothicus*] —Goth'i·cal·ly, *adv.*

b., blend of, blended; c., cognate with; d., dialect, dialectal; der., derived from; f., formed from; g., going back to; m., modification of; r., replacing; s., stem of; t., taken from; ?, perhaps. See the full key on inside cover

ENCYCLOPEDIAS

You have been assigned a term paper. After a mild panic, you go to the library, find the reference collection, and consult a dictionary to make sure you understand the terms in the subject.

Now that you are clear on the subject, you will need something to give you an overview. You need, in other words, a reference book that will summarize the subject so that you can get a handle on it. Here is where encyclopedias enter the picture. They are that excellent overview of the subject, giving the important events, people, and places involved.

"In my library there are several kinds of encyclopedias. Some are only one volume, some are multi-volume sets. Which one should I use?"

The answer to that question is another question. "How much information do you want?"

The one-volume encyclopedia is good for very brief articles; the multi-volume sets will naturally have longer articles, more illustrations, and a helpful list of books on the subject at the end of the article. This list is called a bibliography.

Within the multi-volume sets there is also a difference in the style of writing and the arrangement and amount of coverage devoted to each subject. For example, one of the encyclopedia sets in the reference collection might be the Encyclopedia Britannica. This is a comprehensive encyclopedia; that is, it attempts to give complete coverage to a subject with longer, detailed articles written in a scholarly style. Instead of brief articles on every subject, the Encyclopedia Britannica uses long articles covering broad subject areas.

The Encyclopedia Americana is also a comprehensive encyclopedia, but the style of writing, the length of articles, and the arrangement of the articles are different from the Britannica. Instead of long articles arranged under broad subject areas, the Americana features shorter articles on specific subjects in a dictionary arrangement. Each subject is entered alphabetically beginning with the first volume. For example, the main article about rocks can be found in the Americana in the volume that covers the letter "R," then under the subject "Rocks." The Britannica has no subject entry for "Rocks" in the volume that covers "R." Instead you will find the main article on rocks under the subject "Geology."

Your library may also have encyclopedia sets which are not as scholarly and detailed as Britannica or Americana. Two of these are the World Book Encyclopedia and Compton's Encyclopedia and Fact Index.

So you see, it boils down to how much information you need and the style of writing you prefer.

"O.K., once I've selected one, what's the best way to use it?"

For those encyclopedias which have a dictionary arrangement, with the subjects alphabetically arranged, you only have to look at the backs of the books to see which volume has your subject in it. "A" volume would have subjects beginning with "A," "B" volume covers subjects beginning with the letter "B," and so on. Some encyclopedias use combinations of letters to designate the volumes.

You should be aware, however, that your subject may also be covered under other subject entries. That's why encyclopedias have indexes. The index is either at the end of each volume in the set or in the last volume of the set. The index tells you the volume and page number where each subject is discussed.

To show you how important the index can be, let's take an ordinary subject like "Pecans." It might seem that you would only have to look in the "P" volume for information about pecans.

"Well, why not? After all, how complex can a pecan be?"

Look at the illustration of an encyclopedia index on page 95. The subjects are in heavy dark print. Notice the entry for "Pecan." It is followed by a word in parentheses telling what the subject is. This is followed by the volume number 21 and page number 461, designating the main article on pecans. Notice, however, that pecans are also discussed in volume 20, page 572. And there are the subtopics "Cooking" and "Texas." If you had looked at the first article only, you would have missed a lot of pecans.

Exercise

From the illustration, find the subject entry "Peer and peerage," a term of nobility. Write the volume and page number for the main article. Then list at least two subtopics that discuss this subject.

Volume 21 Page 469
England ; Baron

When using an encyclopedia you must keep in mind its date. You could not expect to find information in an encyclopedia about a recent event or discovery. If it takes several months for a single book to be published, imagine the time involved in publishing a set of twenty-four volumes. Publishers, therefore, use two methods to update the information. One way is to issue a yearbook at the end of each year to cover current events. The other way is to revise the articles with each new printing.

In review, encyclopedias are excellent starting points for term or research papers or for general reading. They provide an overview of the subject, describing the events, people, and places involved. Encyclopedias can be comprehensive in coverage with long detailed articles on broad subject areas or shorter articles on smaller subject areas.

If the subjects are in a dictionary arrangement, they can be found by looking directly in the volume whose letter corresponds with the first letter of the subject. Those that arrange their subjects under broad subject areas are better approached through the index. In both cases it is best to use the index for the fullest coverage of your subject.

ALMANACS

Suppose you had to find the election returns for the last presidential election for Deaf Smith County in Texas or, how about this one, the population growth of U.S. cities from 1900 to 1970? What was the highest and lowest temperature ever recorded in Wisconsin? What was the amount of sales in dollars of all the retail stores in America? Could you find the figure for the total U.S. aid to foreign countries? Who won the Middle Atlantic Conference basketball championship last year?

These might be hard questions to run down if it weren't for a fantastic little reference book called an almanac. Almanacs are excellent for current and past information on just about everything and everyone. They are especially good for sports, politics, education, theater, business, and religion. They provide facts and statistics on governmental agencies, elections, population characteristics, cities and states, the weather and climate, and a host of other important areas of national concern. The information can be in the form of tables, lists, paragraphs, or very brief articles.

The best way to get at what's in an almanac is through the index (located at either the beginning or the end of the book).

Exercise

From the illustration of an almanac index on the following page notice that the subjects are entered in heavy dark print with the page numbers after them. Notice the subject entry "Marriage" and the various subtopics beneath it. From this index tell the subtopic and page number that gives the population of Mexico.

area, capital, population

page 585

ATLASES

"Far away places with strange sounding names." Have you ever longed to visit them? When most people travel to unfamiliar places they use a map to guide them. While you may not visit a lot of far away places there will be times when you will want to know where they are located. An atlas, a collection of maps, is probably where you would look. In addition to the maps of geographical areas, many atlases have articles, charts, tables, and other maps that show the population density, agriculture, climate and weather conditions, vegetation, mineral resources, and principal products of the areas covered.

Because of the variety of areas an atlas can cover it is best to use the index. Most atlases place the index at the end of the volume. In the excerpt from an atlas index on page 99 notice that the cities and towns are entered alphabetically. All entries in the index—whether mountains, lakes, rivers, etc.—will be arranged alphabetically. The page numbers are at the far right. The first city, Pinecroft, Washington, is on page 210. The "D8" is the map index key meaning that Pinecroft is located on the "D" row, column 8, as in the illustration on page 99.

Pinecroft, Wash. D8 210
Pineda, Fla. D6 174
Pinedale, Ariz. C5 168
Pinedale, Wyo. C3 213
Pinega, Sov. Un. C17 41
Pinehurst, Ga. D3 175
Pinehurst, Ida. B2 177

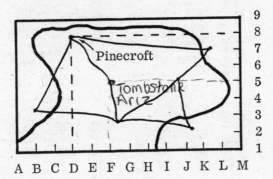

Exercise

From the illustration of an atlas index on page 100, find the map that covers Tombstone, Ariz. Tell the page number, row letter, and column number.

1. Topic ___Tombstone, Ariz.___

2. Page number ___168___

3. Row ___F___

4. Column ___5___

Topaz

MANUALS

Manuals and handbooks are very similar in the service they provide and often it is difficult to tell which is a manual and which is a handbook. The distinction in this guide will be clear cut. Manuals provide guidance or instruction. They tell you how to do something, how to identify something, or how to write in a certain manner. The Chilton Auto Repair Manual gives instruction in auto repair. The Manual of Cultivated Plants helps you identify various plants. A manual that you will probably become acquainted with is the Manual for Writers of Term Papers, Theses, and Dissertations. Manuals can also serve as guides to huge agencies. The U.S. Government Organization Manual, for instance, describes the branches of government, the officials, and their duties

Compilers of manuals try to arrange them to suit the purpose of the publication. The auto repair manuals are arranged by broad subject areas such as "Electrical Systems," "Transmissions," or "Fuel Systems." The table of contents of a manual lists the subjects in the order they are discussed.

Other manuals have indexes like the one illustrated on the next page from A Manual for Writers by Kate L. Turabian. This guide to accepted

Index

style in term or research papers tells you how to outline your paper, cite quotations, prepare footnotes and bibliographies, and so on. In most college courses you must write some formal papers in accordance with a style manual. A guide such as this tells you how to do it correctly. The index helps you pinpoint particular items. The subjects will be in alphabetical order. You can rest assured that a manual such as this will come in handy as you pursue your college career.

Exercise

There is a subject entry in the index shown on page 102 for "Appendix."
What pages cover this subject? _2, 3, 126_

HANDBOOKS

Handbooks, unlike manuals, ordinarily do not guide or instruct. Instead
they provide quick and easy-to-get-to facts. These facts may be in the
form of tables and formulas as in the Handbook of Chemistry, or brief
definitions as in A Handbook of Classical Mythology. All of the subjects
covered in handbooks can, of course, be found in other books. The
whole point of handbooks, though, is that they bring this information
together in an easy-to-consult arrangement in one volume.

Such is the case, for example, with handbooks which identify one of
the most difficult items for students, the appropriate quotation for a
paper or speech. An example is the Home Book of Quotations edited by
Burton Stevenson. The quotations are entered alphabetically by subject
and under each of the subjects alphabetically by author.

The Home Book of Quotations can be used in two ways. If you are
looking for any quotation on a subject, turn directly to the subject and
under it will be the quotations that pertain to the subject. If you already
know the quotation and you want to find the author, go to the concordance
or index of key words.

Suppose you want to find the author of this quotation: "I expect to
pass through this world but once. Any good therefore that I can do or
any kindness that I can show to my fellow creature, let me do it now."
In order to find this quotation and its author, you must first determine
the one key word that identifies the subject of the quotation. In this case
it is "Kindness." Notice in the illustration on page 104 that the first
quotation under "Kindness" is entered as "any k that I can show . . .
1493:6," "k" standing for "kindness." The full quotation is on page 1493,
quotation number 6. The author was one Stephen Grellet.

Often you will not immediately have a quotation in mind but need one
to illustrate a subject. For instance, you could be writing a paper on
"The Importance of Kindness." Using the index again, the subject entry
"Kindness" would direct you to the quotation we looked at, along with
many more.

Finally there is an index of authors which is an alphabetical listing
of authors in the book and the page number of their quotations.

Exercise

From the illustration of the concordance on page 104 find at least one quotation about the great state of Kentucky. Give the page number and quotation number.

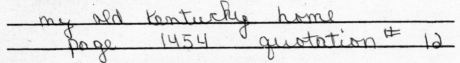

my old Kentucky home

page 1454 quotation # 12

YEARBOOKS

The next two types of reference books are not as common as the others we have looked at. The examples we show, however, are found in most libraries. A yearbook, as you remember, is primarily a compilation of each year's current developments. Encyclopedia publishers use yearbooks to bring the set up to date. Yearbooks may also be issued by various agencies listing the events that occurred in the agency. For instance, the Statistical Abstract of the United States, issued by the U. S. Department of Commerce, Bureau of the Census, is the official statistical report of this agency, summarizing the social, political, and economic developments in the United States. It is probably the best one-volume source for statistics on these subjects. The summary is by chapter headings and includes such topics as population, education, elections, state or local government, finances and employment, transportation, and law.

"'43 must have been a really big year!"

Suppose you wanted to know how each political party voted in the presidential elections over the past fifty years. You simply turn to the index entry "Elections," and the subtopic "Presidential," and there you will find the appropriate page number. The following illustration is an example of how this information is listed. It is a table breaking down the election returns by party, popular vote, and electoral vote from 1900 to 1968.

Vote for President and Representatives   349

No. 547. VOTE CAST FOR PRESIDENT, 1900 TO 1968, AND FOR REPRESENTATIVES, 1930 TO 1970, BY POLITICAL PARTIES

[Prior to 1958, excludes Alaska and Hawaii. Includes vote cast for major party candidates endorsed by minor parties. See also *Historical Statistics, Colonial Times to 1957*, series Y 27–31 and Y 146–149]

YEAR	CANDIDATES FOR PRESIDENT		VOTE CAST FOR PRESIDENT						
	Democratic	Republican	Total popular vote [1]	Democratic			Republican		
				Popular vote		Electoral vote	Popular vote		Electoral vote
				Number	Percent		Number	Percent	
1900	Bryan	McKinley	*1,000* 13,968	*1,000* 6,357	45.5	155	*1,000* 7,218	51.7	292
1904	Parker	T. Roosevelt	13,521	5,084	37.6	140	7,628	56.4	336
1908	Bryan	Taft	14,884	6,412	43.1	162	7,675	51.6	321
1912	Wilson	Taft	15,037	6,297	41.9	435	3,487	23.2	8
1916	Wilson	Hughes	18,531	9,128	49.3	277	8,534	46.1	254
1920	Cox	Harding	26,748	9,130	34.1	127	16,143	60.4	404
1924	Davis	Coolidge	29,086	8,385	28.8	136	15,718	54.0	382
1928	Smith	Hoover	36,812	15,016	40.8	87	21,392	58.1	444
1932	F. D. Roosevelt	Hoover	39,732	22,810	57.4	472	15,759	39.7	59
1936	F. D. Roosevelt	Landon	45,643	27,753	60.8	523	16,675	36.5	8
1940	F. D. Roosevelt	Willkie	49,900	27,313	54.7	449	22,348	44.8	82
1944	F. D. Roosevelt	Dewey	47,977	25,613	53.4	432	22,018	45.9	99
1948	Truman	Dewey	48,794	24,179	49.6	303	21,991	45.1	189
1952	Stevenson	Eisenhower	61,551	27,315	44.4	89	33,936	55.1	442
1956	Stevenson	Eisenhower	62,027	26,023	42.0	73	35,590	57.4	457
1960	Kennedy	Nixon	68,838	34,227	49.7	303	34,108	49.5	219
1964 [2]	Johnson	Goldwater	70,645	43,130	61.1	486	27,178	38.5	52
1968 [2]	Humphrey	Nixon	73,212	31,275	42.7	191	31,785	43.4	301

YEAR	VOTE CAST FOR PRESIDENT—Con.				YEAR	VOTE CAST FOR REPRESENTATIVES [8]				
	Socialist and Soc. Labor	Misc. independent [3]	Prohibition	Communist		Total [9]	Democratic		Republican	
							Number	Percent	Number	Percent
1900	*1,000* 128	*1,000* 56	*1,000* 209	*1,000* –	1930	*1,000* 24,777	*1,000* 11,044	44.6	*1,000* 13,032	52.6
1904	434	117	259	–	1932	37,657	20,540	54.5	15,575	41.4
1908	435	108	254	–	1934	32,256	17,385	53.9	13,558	42.0
1912	929	4,119	206	–	1936	42,886	23,944	55.8	17,003	39.6
1916	599	49	221	–	1938	36,236	17,612	48.6	17,047	47.0
1920	952	334	189	–	1940	46,951	24,092	51.3	21,393	45.6
1924	[4] 36	[5] 4,853	58	[6] 36	1942	28,074	12,934	46.1	14,203	50.6
1928	289	74	20	[6] 21	1944	45,103	22,808	50.6	21,303	47.2
1932	915	63	82	103	1946	34,398	15,221	44.2	18,400	53.5
1936	200	897	38	80	1948	45,933	23,820	51.9	20,920	45.5
1940	131	3	59	46	1950	40,342	19,785	49.0	19,750	49.0
1944	124	147	75	–	1952	57,571	28,605	49.7	28,431	49.4
1948	169	2,351	104	–	1954	42,580	22,347	52.5	20,034	47.0
1952	50	176	73	–	1956	58,426	29,850	51.1	28,449	48.7
1956	46	325	42	–	1958 [10]	45,818	25,733	56.2	19,894	43.4
1960	[4] 48	410	46	–	1960	64,133	35,111	54.7	28,759	44.8
1964 [2]	[4] 45	268	23	–	1962	51,261	26,905	52.5	24,210	47.2
1968 [2]	[4] 53	[7] 10,082	15	1	1964	65,886	37,700	57.2	27,866	42.3
					1966	52,900	26,917	50.9	25,525	48.3
					1968	66,109	33,045	50.0	31,850	48.2
					1970	54,173	28,923	53.4	24,415	45.1

Exercise

Using the illustration on page 106, name Democratic and Republican presidential candidates for the year 1920 and the figure for the total popular vote for that year.

Cox   Harding   26748

DIRECTORIES

A directory is a listing of persons or organizations. It will usually give the addresses, officers, and functions of the organization. Often students need the names of the officers of government agencies or departments. They need the addresses of institutions and societies. Who are the current officers of a particular school district? Who is the president of a firm? These questions are best answered through directories.

One of the most useful directories for students is the Congressional Directory. It is an excellent source for information on all of the branches of congress, listing the officers and personnel of each department, committees, and subcommittees. The biographical section has short sketches of the careers of the congressmen and senators by state. Of particular use are the maps of the congressional districts. This directory is best used through the table of contents for information about the agencies, and through the index for information about individuals.

Exercise

Suppose you need to know the current officers of the Department of the Defense. Under the table of contents entry "Department" and then the subtopic "Defense," you find the page number 485. The illustration on page 108 shows the first page of this article. From the illustration, tell who was the Secretary of the Defense at the time of this writing.

Melvin R. Laird

DEPARTMENT OF DEFENSE

Phones, OXford or Code 11

(All offices located at the Pentagon, Washington, D.C. 20301, unless otherwise stated)

MELVIN R. LAIRD, Secretary of Defense; born in Omaha, Nebr., September 1, 1922, son of Melvin R. and Helen C. Laird; attended Marshfield grade schools and high school; B.A. degree, Carleton College, Northfield, Minn.; served in U.S. Navy, World War II, aboard destroyer *Maddox* in Task Force 58 and Pacific Third Fleet; elected Wisconsin State Senator in 1946; reelected without opposition 1948; member of American Legion, 40 et 8, Veterans of Foreign Wars, Disabled American Veterans, Military Order of Purple Heart, F. & A. M., United Commercial Travelers, and B.P.O.E.; elder, First Presbyterian Church of Marshfield; married Barbara Masters of Indianapolis, Ind., on October 15, 1945; three children—John Osborne, Alison, and David; elected to 83d Congress November 4, 1952; reelected to the 84th, 85th, 86th, 87th, 88th, 89th, 90th, and 91st Congresses; member, House Agricultural Committee, 84th Congress; member, House Appropriations Committee, 83d, 85th, 86th, 87th, 88th, 89th, 90th, and 91st Congresses; served on the following subcommittees; Defense, Health, Education, Welfare, and Labor; resigned from Congress on January 21, 1969; sworn in as Secretary of Defense January 22, 1969.

DAVID PACKARD, Deputy Secretary of Defense, appointed January 24, 1969; born in Pueblo, Colo., September 7, 1912; son of Ella and Sperry S. Packard; graduated from Stanford University, A.B. 1934, E.E. 1939; employed by General Electric Co., Schenectady, N.Y., 1935–38; partner Hewlett-Packard Co., Palo Alto, Calif., 1939–47, president 1947–64, chairman of the board and chief executive officer, 1964–69; married to the former Lucile Salter; four children—David, Nancy, Susan, and Julie.

IMMEDIATE OFFICE OF THE SECRETARY

The Secretary of Defense.—Melvin R. Laird, rm 3E880, Ext. 55261.
  The Special Assistant to the Secretary.—Carl S. Wallace, rm 3E941, Ext. 76351; 8315 Ashwood Drive, Alexandria, Va. 22308.
  Assistant to the Secretary.—William J. Baroody, Jr., rm 3E869, Ext. 77234; 7910 Bolling Drive, Alexandria, Va. 22308.
  Assistant to the Secretary (Legislative Affairs).—Rady A. Johnson, 3216 Patrick Henry Drive, Falls Church, Va. 22044.
  Military Assistant.—Brig. Gen. Robert E. Pursley, USAF, rm 3E880, Ext. 55261; 1008 Westwood Drive, Vienna, Va. 22180.
  Military Assistant.—Rear Adm Daniel J. Murphy, USN, rm 3E880, Ext. 55261; 1600 South Joyce Street, Arlington, Va. 22202.
  Secretary to the Secretary of Defense.—Laura Hawley, rm 3E880, Ext. 55261; 3414 Curtis Drive, Hillcrest Heights, Md. 20023.
  Secretary to the Secretary of Defense.—Thelma E. Stubbs, rm 3E880, Ext. 55261; 1301 South Scott Street, Arlington, Va. 22204.
The Deputy Secretary of Defense.—David Packard, rm 3E921, Ext. 56352.
  Military Assistant.—Col. Raymond B. Furlong, USAF, rm 3E928, Ext. 50661; 6322 Linway Terrace, McLean, Va. 22101.
  Military Assistant.—Col. James G. Boatner, USA, rm 3E928, Ext. 50661; 9121 Volunteer Drive, Alexandria, Va. 22309.
  Secretary to the Deputy Secretary.—Margaret Paull, rm 3E928, Ext. 56352; 1600 South Eads Street, Arlington, Va. 22202.
  Secretary to the Deputy Secretary.—Gwen Kinkead, rm 3E928, Ext. 56352; 2000 South Eads Street, Arlington, Va. 22202.

485

Exercise

As a kind of dry run before the real thing, take this exercise. From the eight types of reference books listed, write the correct one for each question below.

manual ✓   encyclopedia ✓
yearbook —   directory
dictionary ✓   handbook ✓
almanac ✓   atlas ✓

1. For your speech tomorrow you need a good quotation on the subject of love. What type of reference book would have quotations?

   handbook

2. The geography teacher asked you to locate a map which has your hometown. Where would you find the map? _atlas_

3. Another term paper! Before plunging into it, you need a general overview of the subject, a source that would have brief articles telling the important events, people, and places involved. Which reference book do you need? _encyclopedia_

4. The air conditioner in your car broke down, but you could fix it if you had a guide showing what to do. The library has one. What is it called? _manual_

5. What library reference book has the collegiate sports records for your area? _almanac_

6. The government teacher has selected none other than you to tell the class the officers for the Department of Treasury. You race over to the library to consult which reference book? _directory_

7. What in the world does the word "excursus" mean? You could find it in which reference book? _dictionary_

8. What would be a good source for statistics from the U.S. Census Bureau? _yearbook_

Check your answers now on page 126. If you answered these questions correctly, you can skip the post-test. If not, review the information on the questions you missed and take the post-test below. Then, on to the practical work.

POST-TEST

1. Reference books differ from the regular circulating library books in several ways. Name two.

    (a) _They are not read from cover cover_

    (b) _They do not circulate_

2. Reference books come in two distinct classes. Name them.

    (a) _general_

    (b) _Subject_

3. The reference book which gives a broad overview of a subject through brief articles telling the important people, places, and events is called _encyclopaedia_ .

4. The reference book which serves as a guide telling you how to do something is called _a manual_ .

5. The reference book which lists the names and addresses of persons, organizations, or of a particular institution is called

    a directory .

6. The reference book which presents the events of the immediate past year through brief articles, tables, and charts is called

    yearbook .

7. A one-volume source for maps, plates, and charts of geographical areas is called _atlas_ .

8. The reference book that provides information about words, their spelling, meaning, and punctuation is called _dictionary_ .

PRACTICAL WORK

You are ready for some practical work with reference books. For each question we will give you a list of books to use including the Dewey Decimal class number or the Library of Congress class letter of each book. We will abbreviate Dewey with "DC" and Library of Congress with "LC."

You do not have to use books from the given lists. They are only suggestions. Besides, you know there will be others like them in the same area on the reference shelves.

The answers to the questions can be found in the books listed. Many of them will be obvious. For instance, if we ask you to define a political science term and there is a political science dictionary listed, then there is no guess work for you.

We will tell you what subject area the question is in. Use the appropriate subject reference book for that subject to answer it. That's the object of the exercises: to give you the opportunity to use the subject reference books.

Biographies

In locating a biography of someone, you should first try to find out if he is living or dead. Most of the biographical reference books will be devoted to one or the other. Find a biographical sketch of at least <u>one</u> of the people listed below. Use the biographical reference books that we suggest or any similar ones that your library might have. At the time of this writing, all of the persons are living.

Rose Kennedy (American)   Jesse Jackson (American)
Gina Lollobrigida (Italian)   Edward Heath (English)
Andrés Segovia (Spanish)   Arthur Goldberg (American)
Margaret Mead (American)   Pearl Bailey (American)

<u>Current Biography</u> (DC-920. 2; LC-CT100) covers world personalities, with numerous pictures; index in each volume, cumulated to ten years (i. e., 1951–1960 and 1961–1970).

<u>Who's Who in America</u> (DC-920. 073; LC-E663) comes out every two years and covers famous living American men and women.

<u>Who's Who</u> (DC-920. 042; LC-DA28) is almost the same as <u>Who's Who in America</u> except that it covers living Englishmen.

✓<u>Who's Who of American Women</u> (DC-920. 7; LC-CT3260) is the same type of work as the other Who's Whos except that it lists only out-standing American women.

<u>Chambers's Biographical Dictionary</u> (DC-920. 02; LC-CT103) covers the great people of all times of all nations.

<u>International Who's Who</u> (DC-920; LC-CT120) is a listing of the world's most important living people.

Biographical sketch of ___Margaret mead_____

Found in ___Who's Who In the World___ 3rd Ed 1976-1977

Page number ___492_____   Date of birth ___Dec. 16, 1901___

Subject Biographical Dictionaries

Just as there are general biographical dictionaries, so there are subject biographical dictionaries such as <u>Who's Who in American Education</u> for prominent educators or <u>Who's Who in American Politics</u> for governmen-tal figures. Find a biographical sketch on at least <u>one</u> of the people listed on page 113.

Edward William Brooke, U.S. Senator from Massachusetts
Nolan Estes, Superintendent of Schools, Dallas Public School
    System
Clint Murchison, prominent industrialist and businessman
Helen Hayes, noted American theatre actress
Andrew Wyeth, famous American artist
Jonas E. Salk, American doctor, discoverer of polio vaccine
James Arthur Baldwin, best-selling black author
Leonard Bernstein, American conductor and musician

Use the following sources to find your biography. Remember, first
determine what field the person is in, then look down the list of subject
biographical dictionaries and see where it would be found. For example,
a biography of Ethel Waters, famous American actress, would be found
in Who's Who in the Theatre, page 1289, birthdate October 31, 1900.

Who's Who in Science (DC-509.22; LC-Q141)

Who's Who in the Theatre (DC-927.92; LC-PN2012)

The Author's and Writer's Who's Who (DC-928.2; LC-Z2011)

Baker's Biographical Dictionary of Musicians (DC-780.922; LC-ML105)

McGraw-Hill Modern Men of Science (DC-509.22; LC-Q141)

World Who's Who in Commerce and Industry (DC-923.873; LC-HF3023)

Who's Who in American Politics (DC-320.09; LC-E176)

Who's Who in American Education (DC-378.73; LC-LA2311)

Who's Who in American Art (DC-709.22; LC-N6536)

Biographical sketch of ___Leonard Bernstein___
Found in ___Who's Who in music ML106___
Page number ___31___   Date of birth ___1918___

Subject Reference Books: Social Sciences

The social sciences concern the behavior of man as an individual or in groups. Since man is of immense interest to himself, the field is well covered by reference books.

"The trouble with humanity is people."

The social sciences generally include anthropology, economics, religion, history, political science, sociology, criminology, law, philosophy, and psychology.

It would be hard for you to finish college without taking courses in several of these subjects. The social science reference books are easy to use; you will find that they are all of the dictionary, encyclopedia, almanac, and handbook types with which you are already familiar. Look carefully at the list on page 115 of social science reference books. The title will tell you what the book covers and will suggest how the information is arranged. You do not have to use these exact books as there are others like them in each area. Answer at least two of the questions that follow the list of books.

International Encyclopedia of the Social Sciences (DC-300.3; LC-H40) is a seventeen-volume encyclopedia set which deals with important historical and current people and events in the social sciences. The last volume contains the index.

Dictionary of American History (DC-973.03; LC-E174) is a seven-volume set with short articles arranged alphabetically by subject. It is best used by looking up the subject in the index volume (number seven) and then turning to the appropriate page.

Black's Law Dictionary (DC-340.03; LC-KF156) is a one-volume dictionary containing the terms and phrases of American and English law.

American Political Dictionary (DC-320.973; LC-JK9) is a one-volume dictionary that explains American political terms and concepts. The information is presented in chapters, each covering an important segment in American politics. It is best used through the index in the back of the book.

Unger's Bible Dictionary (DC-220.3; LC-BS440) is a one-volume dictionary emphasizing historical, geographical, doctrinal, and archaeological aspects of the Bible.

Using the subject reference books listed above, or any like them, answer any two of the following questions. Remember, look at each question and decide which reference book would cover it. Be sure you put the title of the book and page number where you found the answer.

1. Explain the political term "split ticket."   *pg. 119   LC-JK9   Voting for candidates of two or more parties for different offices.*

2. Briefly explain the Kansas-Nebraska Act.   *p. 1836   A compromise Bill attempting to solve the problem of slavery in new territories*

3. Where would you find a good definition of marriage from a social science point of view? _____

4. An important term in law is "breach of contract." Explain very
   briefly what it means. _____

   _____

   _____

   _____

5. What is another term for the religious concept of the "Holy Spirit"?

   _____

6. Find an article on the social aspects of suicide. Tell the title of the
   book and the page number. _____

   _____

Subject Reference Books: Language and Literature

This section of the reference collection contains works on foreign languages, English language usage, quotations, authors and their works.
The volumes cover the same type of questions that the majority of you
will have to answer when you take an English or foreign language course
at some time during your academic career. Look at the reference
books carefully and decide which will supply the answer to the exercise
questions.

A Library of Literary Criticism: Modern American Literature. (DC-
810.904; LC-PS221) is a three-volume set, alphabetically listing
modern American authors and containing criticism of their main
works. To use it, simply find your author alphabetically by his last
name and you will see a list of criticisms of his work.

American Authors, 1600-1900, a Biographical Dictionary (DC-928.1;
LC-PS21) is an alphabetical listing of American authors who died
before 1900. To use this reference book, determine the author's
date, look up by his last name. This book also contains a list of
each author's works and their dates.

Twentieth Century Authors, a Biographical Dictionary (DC-928; LC-PN
771) is a one-volume work with a supplement, containing biographies
of twentieth century authors and their main works with the dates. To
use it, look up the author by his last name.

Familiar Quotations (DC-808.88; LC-PN6081) is a book of quotations
listed under the name of the person who originated them, with
authors listed chronologically by birthdate. A subject index and a
first line index are at the back of the book. To use, either look
under the author in the main part of the book or look under the subject or first line in the index. *Dewey* *Library* *congress*

The New Cassell's German Dictionary (DC-433.2; LC-PF3640),
Cassell's Spanish Dictionary (DC-463.2; LC-PC4640), and
Cassell's French Dictionary (DC-443.2; LC-PC2640) are all foreign
language dictionaries. To use, simply look up the word to find
the foreign language meaning.

Since it is almost certain that you will have to answer these types of
questions in your classes, you must answer three of the questions below.

1. Translate the word "book" into either French, German, or Spanish.
   Libro *libro*   *Ref. PC 4640.C35*
                                      1966
   Dictionary used *Cassell's Spanish Dictionary*

2. One of the authors whose works you will probably read at some time
   is John Steinbeck. Find a biographical sketch of him. Give the date
   that Tortilla Flat was written. *1935*
   Reference book used *Twentieth Century Authors*
                              Ref. PN 771.K86

3. A quotation from Lord Byron on the subject of love is "Man's love is
   of man's life a part; it is woman's whole existence." This is from
   which work by Byron? *Don Juan Canto I*
   Reference book used *Familiar Quotations - John Bartlett*
                              Ref. PN 6081.B27 1955

4. Nathaniel Hawthorne, who died in 1864, was a great American author.
   Find a biographical sketch of him and tell when The Scarlet Letter
   was written. _____
   Reference book used _____

5. Stephen Crane is the American author of The Red Badge of Courage.
   Find a criticism of this book and tell the reference book and the page
   where you found it. Book used _____
   _____ Page number _____

Subject Reference Books: Fine Arts

The fine arts include music, drama, art, and dance. You may never take a course in the fine arts but someday you may want to sing, dance, act, or paint. The reference books in fine arts may not help you sing and dance any better, but they can help you answer questions in those fields. You should have little trouble answering the questions as you are by now skilled in using the reference type of book.

Grove's Dictionary of Music and Musicians (DC-780.3; LC-ML100) is a ten-volume set covering every phase of music. Items are arranged in dictionary style by the subject. To use this reference book, look in the volume in which your subject falls alphabetically.

McGraw-Hill Dictionary of Art (DC-703; LC-N33) is a five-volume set, dictionary arranged. To use, look under the volume in which your subject falls alphabetically.

The World of Great Composers (DC-927.8; LC-ML390) is a selected list of great musicians with information on each. Use the index at the end of the book to find page numbers for your subject.

American Negro Art (DC-709.73; LC-N6538) is a book of black artists and their works. To find an example of an artist's work, use the first index, called "Artists and Pictures."

The Praeger Picture Encyclopedia of Art (DC-703; LC-N5300) is an encyclopedia which has entries by subject, alphabetically. It also has an index. This book covers art, architecture, sculpture, etc.

There are, of course, other reference books in the fine arts sections located in the same areas. Answer any one of the questions below using one of the fine arts reference books.

1. In music what is a "pentatonic scale"? _____

_____

2. In the art world, what does the term "emulsion" mean? _____

_____

3. When and where was the famous pianist Franz Liszt born? _He_
1811 - 1886

was born in Raiding, Hungary
ML390.E86

4. A reproduction of a painting of the black artist Archbald Motley might be found in which reference book? _____

Subject Reference Books: Science and Technology

This is a very important area in the reference collection. It is here
that the chemistry, biology, physics, mathematics, electricity, nursing, and the technical reference books are located. Most of these are
of the types you are now very familiar with—the subject dictionary or
encyclopedia. Moreover, many manuals and handbooks will supply information in the form of graphs, statistics, charts, and formulas.
Again, look at the reference books carefully and decide which book
would have the answer you need.

Computer Dictionary (DC-657.803; LC-QA76.15.S512) is a dictionary-
   arranged work which lists the words and topics alphabetically.

Encyclopedia of the Biological Sciences (DC-574.03; LC-QH13) is an
   encyclopedia of biology, alphabetically arranged by subject. To
   use it, turn to the index in the back of the book to find the location
   of your subject.

Dorland's Illustrated Medical Dictionary (DC-610.3; LC-R121) is a
   dictionary of medical terms alphabetically arranged.

Modern Dictionary of Electronics (DC-621.381; LC-TK7804) includes
   electronic terms discussed in dictionary form.

Chilton's Auto Repair Manual (DC-629.28; LC-T1152) is a manual on
   automobile repair in three sections: "Car Section," "Unit Repair
   Section," and "Trouble Shooting Section." Automobiles are listed
   alphabetically by their names.

McGraw-Hill Encyclopedia of Science and Technology (DC-503; LC-Q
   121) is a fifteen-volume set covering most subjects in science and
   technology. Volume 15 is the index; better start there.

Using the reference books described above, answer at least two of
these science and technology reference questions.   3

1.) We have all heard of people who need to count calories. What is the

scientific meaning of the word "calorie"? _A unit of_
heat, the amount of heat required
to raise the temp. of 1 gram of water from
_14.5 C to 15.5 C_
Reference book used _Dorlands Illustrated_
medical Dictionary 54th Ed
Ref. R. 121.D73

2. In computer or data processing language, what is a "program"?

_____

_____

Reference book used _____

3. Using a biological encyclopedia or dictionary, give a brief definition
of bacteria. _____

_____

Reference book used _____

4. Find a definition of the medical term "hematosis." *The
formation of the blood. The
aeration of the blood in the lungs.*
Reference book used *Dorland's Illustrated
medical Dictionary Ref R 121 .D73*

5. A coulomb is an electrical term. Find a definition of it. *The
quantity of electricity which
passes any point in an electric
circuit in 1 sec., when the current*
Reference book used *Modern Dictionary of
Electronics Ref TK 7804 .H6*

6. Where would you find information on the engine of a 1971 Mercury?

Name the reference work and the page where the information begins.

Reference book _____

Page number _____

*is maintained constant at
1 ampere.*

Take a break!

Book Review Digest

Many term and research papers and library assignments require book reviews. Often book reviews are difficult to locate, as they are normally not indexed in the periodical indexes with which you are familiar. Fortunately, there is a reference source that does locate book reviews. It is called the Book Review Digest.

Look at that title again—Book Review Digest! It does not say Book Review Index or Dictionary of Book Reviews or even Encyclopedia of Book Reviews, does it? In other words, it obviously is something different from the reference books that you have been using.

Sure enough, Book Review Digest is a listing of digests of book reviews, entered alphabetically by the names of the authors of the books. A digest is a shortened or condensed version of the book review, not the actual and entire review. You need only know three things about your book to use the Book Review Digest—the author's last name, the title, and the year of publication.

Author of book ──────────→

Title ──────

Paragraph briefly explains
what book is about ──────→

First book review digest:
The entire book review is
in <u>Library Journal</u>, Vol.
90, page 128, January 1,
1965 and is 150 words long.

Check periodical card file
to see if this periodical
is available at your library.

Second book review digest:
The whole review is found
in <u>New York Times Book
Review</u>, page 4, February
21, 1965, and is 170 words
long.

HUGO, RICHARD F. Death of the Kapowsin tavern. 55p $3.95 Harcourt
811   Puget Sound area—Poetry   65-11990
"The wilderness of the Pacific Northwest where loggers and fishermen ply their trade and rest their bones along lakes and rivers whose names—Kapowsin, Duwamish, Skagit, Hoh-rise out of a primal Indian past provides setting and theme for many of the poems in this . . . volume. . . . The title piece . . . laments the end of a tavern where trollers with the night chill of the lake upon them could go for 'bad wine/washed down frantically with beer.'" (Publisher's note) Some of these poems appeared previously in various periodicals and four appear in Five Poets of the Pacific Northwest, an anthology [BRD 1965]. The author is a member of the Department of English at Montana State University in Missoula.

"Frequently the base of a poem turns on war experiences and diverse places. The poems share a probing of mortality, the mystery of memory and the mockery of man by wind, fire and dissolution. The poetry itself offers a metamorphosis, as, on an antique plate, 'a rose survives the cracks.' This collection of brittle, brooding verse will appeal to those sophisticated enough to be untroubled by frank, occasionally unconventional language. Recommended for university and large public library collections." J. R. Willingham
Library J 90:128 Ja 1 '65 150w
"Richard Hugo is a sort of square's Gary Snyder. Perhaps it's the subject, the woods and mountains and rivers of the Pacific Northwest. All of us who've lived and worked there sound alike when we write about it. It's not just local color. That country does something to your blood, to your sensibility and your senses. Then too, 'Death of the Kapowsin Tavern is, of all [the] books, a record of the hardest struggle for a unique syntax—'This is me, Hugo, speaking and nobody else.' He is a tough-minded man, not just a success as a poet, a professor, or a worker at Boeing Aircraft; you gain from the fiber of his poems the feeling he'd make out, whatever he set his hand to. John Ciardi is the only other contemporary poet I can think of who conveys so strongly the sense of being at home in the world." Kenneth Rexroth
N Y Times Bk R p4 F 21 '65 170w
Reviewed by Mark McCloskey
Poetry 107:125 N '65 350w
"These poems take startling risks with language, and even where they fail they persuade us that the risks have been worth the taking. . . . The language, even when in its excess it turns affected and hectic, seems to follow the very curves and mouldings of experience itself. But if Hugo's technique dazzles, his themes disappoint: his confrontations with sinister places, flowing waters, and the perpetual mystery of fecundity become repetitive, and his obsessions with the losses of the past come finally to seem unfresh, automatic." Paul Fussell
Sat R 48:30 Jl 3 '65 400w
"These poems are ugly poems often, but of an ugliness which is its own beauty, a human beauty not of form and grace but of action and passion. His discovery of beauty in violence and ugly disaster is the vision of a poet of intense insight; Richard F. Hugo, too, is a poet of skill matching that vision."
Va Q R 41:cxxi autumn '65 60w

HUIE, WILLIAM BRADFORD. Three lives for Mississippi. 254p pl $4.95 WCC bks. 230 W. 41st st. N.Y. 18; for sale by Affiliated pubs.
301.45 Goodman, Andrew, Chaney, James Earl. Schwerner, Michael Henry. Murder. Race Problems. Mississippi—Race question   65-19585
The author is "a journalist. . . . He first of all sketches the life of Michael Schwerner, son of a New York wig manufacturer and oldest of the three civil rights workers slain near Philadelphia, Miss., in June of 1964, and then reconstructs the circumstances of the murder and the progress of its investigation in a community that approved it. In the first part, he is fascinated by the idealism of Schwerner. . . . In the second part, he studies the mind of the Klansman who can commit atrocities with his hand on the Bible." (America)

"One gets the impression that both mentalities [the idealism of Schwerner and the mind of the Klansman] are equally paradoxical for

Page 122 is an illustration taken from the <u>Book</u> <u>Review</u> <u>Digest</u>. Notice the excerpt is titled <u>Book</u> <u>Review</u> <u>Digest</u> 1965, and it contains digests of books reviewed in 1965. The first entry is the author's last name, in heavy dark print—HUGO, RICHARD F. The title is next, <u>Death</u> <u>of</u> <u>the</u> <u>Kapowsin</u> <u>Tavern</u>, followed by the number of pages in the book, the price, and publisher. Beneath this is a paragraph telling what the book is about. We then come to the first book review digest. You can see that it is a very brief paragraph, yet it is a digest of a 150–word review.

"Good grief, how do I know all of this?"

At the end of the digest, there is in dark print <u>Library</u> J 90:128 Ja 1 '65 150w. That tells you that this is a digest of a review which appeared in <u>Library</u> <u>Journal</u>, volume 90, page 128, January 1, 1965, and the actual review is 150 words. Each <u>Book</u> <u>Review</u> <u>Digest</u> volume has a subject and title index at the end. A cumulative volume is published every five years.

Exercise

Using the illustration on page 124 find a digest of a review of Anthony Herbert's book, <u>Soldier</u>. There is a list of abbreviations used in each issue of <u>Book</u> <u>Review</u> <u>Digest</u>. Since it is not shown, write the abbreviations of the periodical if you cannot determine its title.

Title of periodical ____Nat. R._____

Volume number __25__ Page review is found on __321__

Date of periodical _3-16-73_

Number of words of the review __850__

terms—even if the author does not always avoid being patronizing. The musical examples are mostly quite playable . . . though it can sometimes be difficult to see their immediate relevance because of the seemingly haphazard layout; one may have to look several pages farther on or back for the reference in the text."
TLS p1326 O 22 '71 200w

HENDIN, DAVID. Death as a fact of life. 255p $7.50 '73 Norton
128 Death
ISBN 0-393-08540-6   LC 72-8883
The author discusses death and dying and some of the moral, ethical and scientific issues involved in our current attitudes toward death. Contents include revising the criteria of death; transplants, doctors and death; children and death; grief and bereavement, the ecology of dying, and related topics. Bibliography, Index.

Reviewed by Fred Rotondaro
Best Sell 32:494 F 1 '73 450w
"This wide-ranging book discusses such controversial issues as the morality of euthanasia, the dilemma of informing patients or withholding from them the prognosis of death, the definition of death, the ethics of freezing bodies after death for possible later restoration to life, and the increasing need for urban land devoted to cemeteries. . . . The most valuable feature of this volume is its appeal to lay audiences who desire an interesting, easy-to-read, but accurate account of the topic of death." B. J. Kalisch
Library J 98:171 Ja 15 '73 160w
"Death, like sex, is an old taboo subject that is taboo no longer. And David Hendin has made use of the new freedom he feels to write frankly and clinically about the dead and dying, which, of course, includes all of us. Death isn't as much fun as sex, but it is just as fascinating. . . . Hendin, a New York science editor who has written three other books on popular medicine, offers a chapter on each of several familiar deadly subjects. . . . It is all quite engrossing and not that depressing; it's sort of refreshing to slough off all those taboos. [The author] is a capable reporter. . . . He is full of macabre facts and to his credit stays completely away from matters outside his competence. The reader will have to find out for himself about the hereafter." David Sanford
N Y Times Bk R p16 F 25 '73 900w

HENKEL, STEPHEN C. Bikes; a how-to-do-it guide to selection, care, repair, maintenance, decoration, safety, and fun on your bicycle; il. by the author. 96p $4.95 '72 Chatham press; for sale by Viking
796.6 Bicycles and bicycling—Juvenile literature
SBN 85699-033-7   LC 73-172354
This book is a "guide to help young and old alike through each step from buying a bike and learning to ride it to working those ten-speed gears, or making an old favorite run like new. . . . Advice on what is the best size bike for you, special tools, games, safety on the road, and even a little history is included." (Publisher's note) Bibliography, Index. "Grade seven and up." (Library J)

"A comprehensive treatment of bikes and bicycling containing clear, concise, accurate information. . . . Although the price information will become dated, this does not detract from the book's overall value. The illustrations are labeled and easy to follow." E. C. Sanborn
Library J 98:654 F 15 '73 80w
"[Here] is a flat-format all-around bike book, handy for laying flat while following instructions; it offers advice on everything. . . . It's partly aimed at the 10-speed freaks and partly at the banana-seat-set. This may be the book for Pop to leave around hoping someone will get interested in fixing up all the inoperative wheel toys in the garage; not that most adults couldn't make good use of it." H. C. Gardner
N Y Times Bk R p8 Je 4 '72 70w

HENN, T. R. The living image; Shakespearean essays. 147p $8 '72 Barnes & Noble
822.3 Shakespeare, William—Criticism, interpretation, etc.
SBN 416-66220-X LC [72-193616]
In this study of Shakespeare's imagery, "seven essays are on fowling, hunting, fishing, horsemanship, archery, and military weapons and tactics in the plays; the eighth concerns

images in Antony and Cleopatra." (Choice) Bibliography, Index.

"[Henn's] chief and solid contribution lies in the material in the sporting and military essays which he draws from his experiences as a boy in Ireland. He knows at first hand about hawks and hounds, fish, horses, guns, traps, and bows and arrows. Fresh light is turned on these subjects in the plays, clearing up the meaning of difficult lines, particularly concerning hunting. His pages on the last scene in Antony and Cleopatra are excellent. He includes many good references to surviving customs and to modern writers, especially Yeats. Graceful, clear, informal style—anything but pedantic."
Choice 9:1446 Ja '73 150w
"[The chapter on the Elizabethan army and its organization] is packed with interesting information. It not only illuminates many individual passages of the plays, but gives also a panoramic survey of Elizabethan military life. Dr Henn thus brings fresh interest to an area of the drama which has receded in immediacy from modern audiences (to the point where stage battles embarrass producers) though it fascinated contemporaries. . . . These essays have obviously been written con amore and will be read with as much pleasure as profit (though possibly the author's unashamed relish for his subject may offend pacifists and opponents of blood-sports)."
TLS p517 My 5 '72 300w

HERBERT, ANTHONY B. Soldier [by] Anthony B. Herbert; with James T. Wooten. 498p pl $7.95 '73 Holt
959.704 Vietnamese Conflict, 1961- — Personal narratives. U.S. Army
ISBN 0-03-091456-6   LC 72-78121
In this account of his military career the author focuses on the corruption and negligence of the U.S. Army in Vietnam. He claims that his superior officers, the "commander and deputy commander of [his] Vietnam unit . . . had refused to investigate or act upon eight incidents of murder, torture or mistreatment of prisoners he called to their attention." (Newsweek) Index.

"Former Lieutenant Colonel Herbert is the highly decorated, widely experienced career officer whose complaints about military misconduct in Vietnam got him prematurely retired from the service. Minus the sword, the colonel has taken up the pen and produced a mixture of autobiography and diatribe. Both are readable and passionate, and it is no easy matter to disentangle the two. One thing, however, is clear; the book is not designed for the encouragement or consolation of pacifists. The author has no objection to brutality, or to killing. He merely wants to see them applied efficiently to proper military targets." Phoebe Adams
Atlantic 231:103 F '73 110w
Reviewed by Leon Lindsay
Christian Science Monitor p9 Ja 31 '73 350w
"[When this book attempts] to be philosophic about things military, what comes out is usually either painful or comic. . . . The writing . . . reeks with profanity and obscenity. Vulgarity, if not a way of life with Mr. Herbert, is a conversational crutch. When he recounts dialogue with his superiors, or repeats what he said to troops the smut is always present. He lays it on thick elsewhere in his writing. . . . As for . . . the reliability of Mr. Herbert's testament, it his recollection of what happened around Ankhe and Tuyhoa in Vietnam is no better than his recall of experience in Korea, the grading should be zero minus. Having been there at the time, moving through the same scenes with the same outfits, I say that he dilates expansively on things that never happened." S. L. A. Marshall
Nat R 25:321 Mr 16 '73 850w
Reviewed by Crawford Woods
New Repub 168:24 F 24 '73 1900w
Reviewed by J. G. Gray
N Y Times Bk R p2 F 18 '73 800w
New Yorker 49:130 Mr 17 '73 210w
"[This] salty autobiography, written with the help of The New York Times reporter who covered Herbert's war with the Army from his filing charges in March 1971 to his bitter resignation last year, is apt to induce apoplexy among its readers in the Pentagon. Herbert's sardonic portrayal of a demoralized, and demoralizing, military effort in Vietnam is presented from a particularly intimate and damaging perspective. . . . This hard-bitten combat veteran may also be suspected of exaggerating, in retrospect, his innocent outrage at field brutalities. . . . Yet given a choice between

ANSWERS TO PRE-TEST AND POST-TEST

1. (a) Reference books are normally not read from cover to cover like the regular circulating library books.
   (b) Reference books do not circulate.
   (c) They are not shelved with the regular circulating books, but in a reference collection or reference room.
   (d) Reference books have an "R" or "REF" above the call number on the catalog entries and on the book.
2. (a) general reference books
   (b) subject reference books
3. an encyclopedia
4. a manual
5. a directory
6. a yearbook
7. an atlas
8. a dictionary

ANSWERS TO EXERCISES

Page 89

1. almanac
2. atlas
3. directory
4. manual

5. yearbook
6. dictionary
7. encyclopedia
8. handbook

Page 91

The word "gospel" is most often a noun meaning "the body of doctrine taught by Christ and the apostles" or "glad tidings." It has other meanings and sometimes it is an adjective.

Page 94

The main article for the subject "Peer and peerage" is found in volume 21, page 469. The first two subtopics are "Baron" (volume 3, page 259) and "Baronet" (volume 3, page 259).

Page 96

The population of Mexico can be found under the subject entry "Mexico," subtopic "Area, capital, population," page 585.

Page 99

1. Tombstone, Ariz.   3. F
2. page 168   4. 5

Page 103

Pages 2, 3, and 126 deal with the subject "Appendix."

Page 105

The first quotation about Kentucky is on page 1847, quotation 2.

Page 107, top

The Democratic presidential candidate for 1920 was Cox, the Republican was Harding.   There was a total popular vote of 26,748,000.

Page 107, bottom

The Secretary of the Defense at the time of this writing was Melvin R. Laird.

Page 109

1. handbook   5. almanac
2. atlas   6. directory
3. encyclopedia   7. dictionary
4. manual   8. yearbook

"... and over here is our rare book collection."

CHAPTER FOUR
Library Services

"Service is our most important product," says the advertising slogan of one company. It could also be the slogan for libraries because one of the main reasons for their existence is to serve the informational needs of the patrons. A library offers more than a book collection, periodicals, and reference books. As you read through these additional services, try to find out how and where your library offers each service and write it in the blank spaces provided.

CIRCULATION DEPARTMENT

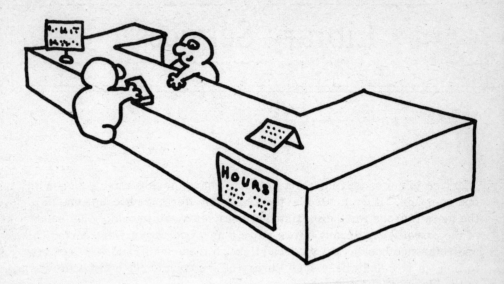

Did you know that in the first college libraries, students were not permitted to borrow the books? There is evidence that the librarians actually tried to "protect" the books from the students. Times have changed and so have libraries. Rather than protect the books from students librarians are doing everything they can to help students get the books they need. The circulation desk is where books are checked out.

Libraries have different ways to check out materials. Some of the circulation procedures are completely automated and you only have to present a student identification card with the book. For others you must write the book information on a check-out slip. One of the best ways to learn how your library checks out books is to <u>do it</u>. If there is no information available telling you what to do, the library clerks at the desk will be glad to show you.

When you check the book out, there will be a loan period stamped somewhere on the book. If you don't see it, be sure to ask. Normally books can be borrowed for two weeks, but it is a good idea to make sure. If you keep the book longer than the loan period, some libraries charge fines and if they are not paid your grades can be held up until the fine is paid. But don't worry; the fine is usually very small—unless you let it get out of hand. There really is no need to have a fine as books can usually be renewed for at least one loan period.

Finally, learn the hours that the library is open. Most are open from the first class period until the last, but some are also open on weekends. Now, why don't you find out the following things about your library?

Circulation procedure (How do you check books out?) *checked out with a currently valid student identification card.*

Loan period and renewals *circulate for a period of 3 weeks renewed in person with ID card*

Library hours ___ 8-10 ___ 8-5 ___ 2-6 ___

Days open ___ M-Th ___ Fri ___ Sun ___

REFERENCE DEPARTMENT

From using this guide, you have learned to use the various types of reference books. There will be times, however, when you simply cannot find the answers or locate material on your subject. Ask the reference librarian for help. In one college, the librarians tell the students at orientation to look for materials by themselves for 20 to 30 minutes. If after that time they cannot find what they need, they should ask for help. This is a pretty good idea. Don't become frustrated. Try to find your materials by yourself, but don't beat a dead horse! Ask for help. Some libraries will have large reference departments with several reference librarians available; others will have a smaller staff with perhaps only one librarian. Get to know your reference librarians; they want to know you.

If your library has a reference desk, where is it located? *the Reference desk is located 2nd floor Straight ahead as you come up stairs*

What is the name of the reference librarian? *the Ref. Lib. is Patricia Srodell also assistant Director Ms. Heintzberger, Mrs. Davis*

RESERVE BOOKS

Have you ever been assigned a chapter in a book which, when you went to the library to find it, had been checked out? To combat this, teachers will place certain books and materials "on reserve"—that is, they are reserved for very short loan periods ranging from several hours to several days. You can appreciate this, particularly when you go to the reserve desk or reserve room and find the book that you need for an assignment or learn that it is to be returned in a short time. Why not ask the teacher if the next reading assignment has been placed on reserve?

Where is the reserve desk or room located in your library? _____

Reserve materials found at circulation desk.

What are the loan periods? *limited circulation up to three days*

BROWSING BOOKS AND PAPERBACKS

Are you one of those people who love to curl up with a good novel?
What about reading the book on that movie you just saw? Many libraries
have a browsing collection of new titles received and popular fiction.
You may also find a paperback collection of current popular books.
These books should be a part of your education just like the required
reading or research reading. Robert Louis Stevenson noted that "The
most influential books, and the truest in their influence, are works of
fiction . . . . They repeat, they rearrange, they clarify the lessons
of life; they disengage us from ourselves, they constrain us to the
acquaintance of others; and they show us the web of experience . . . ."

Where is the browsing collection located in your library? *It is located on the first floor to the right as you come into LRC.*

INFORMATION OR PAMPHLET FILE

An excellent source for company reports and reports from state and
local governmental agencies is an information or pamphlet file. Some
libraries also clip newspaper articles on important current events.
Often this file can contain information on subjects that cannot be
located from books and periodicals. Most of these files are arranged
alphabetically by subject.

Where is the information or pamphlet file? *In the*
Reference department

COLLEGE CATALOGS

If you are a high school student planning to attend college, a junior
college student graduating to a four-year college, or an undergraduate
intending to get a masters degree, right now is not too soon to visit the
college catalog section of a library. You should find out the admission
requirements, course programs, degree requirements, grants and
scholarships available, and all of the information associated with the
college. If you are, for example, a junior college student expecting
to attend a four-year college, you want to know now that the courses
you are taking will be applicable to the four-year college program.

Where is the college catalog section in your library? *In room*
205 & 206 in the Opportunity Room
(Career Info. & College Catalogs)
2nd floor near reference Desk (to the
left of desk if you are facing it)

MICROFORMS

Have you ever had periodicals or newspapers pile up at your home?
You hate to throw them away but they soon fill up your book cases and
boxes. Libraries have the same problem except on a greater scale.
Libraries cannot throw them away as they are a valuable source for
research. One way to cope with the problem of accumulating and stor-
ing back issues of periodicals and newspapers is to acquire them in
microform. The most widely used microform is microfilm. "Micro"
means very small. The periodicals are photographed or microphotographed onto film. Each roll of microfilm will contain issues of periodicals for a certain period. One roll, for example, contains the February 1, 1948 to February 1, 1949 issues of Time magazine. To use
microfilm you need to know the date of the periodical and then find the
corresponding roll of microfilm that contains that issue. The rolls of
microfilm will be in boxes with the dates typed on them.

"How do I use the microfilm once I find the roll that has my issue in it?"

Libraries that have microfilm will also have a microfilm reader. The reader enlarges the microfilm back to a size that you can read. The microfilm roll is very easy to thread onto the reader. You will probably need to be shown how to use the reader the first time but after that, in most libraries you are allowed to put the microfilm on the reader yourself. Many libraries will also have a microfilm reader-printer which will photocopy any article on microfilm.

There are several other microforms which your library may have; microfiche and microcards are some. They all contain microphotographed materials. If you need help in locating and using the microforms or readers, just ask for help. You'll be amazed at how eager librarians are to assist you in using microforms.

Where are the microforms located in your library? _Second_
Floor ; Microfilm Rm 227-229
Micro copiers Same area
Where are the microfilm readers? _Throughout library_
1st 2nd floor near rm. 203 & 202
upstairs
Is there a reader-printer? If so, how much does it cost to use? ___
Micro copiers ; 10¢ per page

TYPING ROOMS

Many libraries furnish typing rooms where manual or electric typewriters can be used for a small fee. Like the photocopiers, they help
you save time. You do not have to take notes from library resources
in longhand, then type them up at home. Type them directly from the
resource. Be sure to return the books and periodicals to the area that
they came from when you finish.

Where is the typing room located? *Second floor of
LRC in room 221 A*

How much does it cost to use the typewriters? *Manuals - free
Electric -   Or bring your own!
30 min. = 10¢
1 hr. = 25¢*

TELEPHONE DIRECTORIES

"Dang it, I just can't remember the phone number of that girl
upstate!"
  You can, of course, call information, but you can also look up any
number in the telephone directories that libraries keep. The larger
libraries will have out-of-state directories. Smaller libraries may
only have the directories for major cities in your state.

Where are the telephone directories? *On the first
floor along the hallway near
the restrooms*

DISPLAYS

Libraries are proud of their displays. Many will have a different display each month. A lot of time and thought have gone into them. Take
a look at the display cases as you use the library. They may contain
everything from a collection of past American election buttons to rare
and valuable books.

Where are the display cases? *Near the Control
Exit desk as you are going
out they are to the left of
the desk!*

PHOTOCOPIERS

Suppose you have found the materials you need for a library assignment
but don't have the time to read it or take notes on it. Take a picture of
it! That's right, photocopy it. For a very small amount of money you
can have a copy of any magazine article, an assignment on reserve, or
a section of a book. Please don't destroy a library resource by cutting
it or stealing it. It just isn't necessary. Use the photocopiers.

You can also use a photocopier to copy a friend's class notes if you
have been absent. There is no need to fall behind because you missed a
few days.

Where is the photocopier in your library? ___Second floor___
___In room 221___

How much does it cost per copy? ___10¢ per page___

It'll 'tear you up' to find this guy's been at work on something you are reading.

STUDY CARRELS

Most libraries have study carrels which are partially enclosed desks.
They are for individual study. If you have a hard time concentrating
when you read or study, use these carrels. They help block out noise
and the distraction of people passing by. Some libraries place them in
one area, others spread them out over the building.

Where does your library have the study carrels? _On second_
floor near west end of library.

AUDIO-VISUAL MATERIALS

You know that a library is a source for information. A very important
part of that information is the audio-visual materials. Many libraries
themselves are part of a learning center which houses the printed
materials (books, periodicals, etc.) and non-printed or audio-visual
materials (slides, tapes, films, records, etc.). This learning center—
called the learning resource center or information resources center—
exposes students to different methods of learning. Many teachers supplement their lectures with films, television programs, tape recordings,
and phonograph records. Some courses are taught entirely, or in part,
with slides and tapes, computer-assisted devices, or other electronic
media. It is possible then in one course to hear a stimulating lecture
by the teacher, have a library assignment to read a chapter in a book
about a particular aspect of the lecture, and then see a film or listen to
a record or tape which further highlights the lecture—not all in one day,
of course.

One library handbook describes the audio-visual materials like this:

Go Ape with Tape

There's another section of the Learning Resource
Center that they call the Programmed Learning Center.
All this really means is that your instructor can give
you extra help without taking up class time. There are
special booths for listening to tapes and looking at TV
tapes. You can also check out the equipment to make
your own tapes and there are special, closed-in areas
so you won't be disturbed. The people in this section
are friendly, too, so don't panic—they'll help you.

If you have an assignment to use the audio-visual materials be sure
to ask your teacher to explain exactly what you are to use, what form it
is (tapes, records, films), the title of the material, and where it is
located.

RULES AND REGULATIONS

Perhaps the less said about "rules and regulations" the better. You know, however, that all institutions must have some. We like the way one library handled them. The following "Library Bill of Rights" was taken from a library handbook written by students.

Your Library Bill of Rights

1. Contrary to popular belief, we don't discourage conversation in the library—just leave your megaphones outside!
2. If you need popcorn, cokes, candy, sandwiches, or any other staffs of life while you are studying—use the snack bar—we're trying to keep down the ants.
3. You can check out anything we've got that circulates— just get it in on time. If you don't we can always use the money (5¢ per day).
4. If someone refuses to let you study in peace, tell a librarian. They keep a gorilla locked up in the back for just such occasions.
5. This is a library—a library that is—so . . . feel free! But don't go ape (leave that to the gorilla in the back— it's his bag)!

Thank you

LIBRARY STAFF

Probably the most valuable service a library can offer is a well trained staff eager to help their patrons make effective use of the library. Your library offers that service. Take them up on it. It was the aim of this guide to teach you the basics in library use. Hopefully we have succeeded. But there will be times when you cannot find the materials you need or locate a particular library service. Ask the library staff to help you. If you like the service that you have received at the library, tell the staff. They would appreciate hearing from you.

"What if the library doesn't have what I need?"

Most libraries are glad to have your suggestions for possible purchases. If you need the material immediately, try your public library. In fact you should get a public library card as soon as possible.

Your library however may provide an interlibrary loan service where they will borrow from other libraries the materials that you need.

Like we said, "Service is our most important product."

Writing a Research Paper

For many students a term or research paper is an agonizing burden. Some will avoid an otherwise interesting course with a good teacher simply because they have heard that he assigns research papers. This is unfortunate because, like anything else, once you learn the proper way to write a paper it becomes routine and no longer a great bugaboo. There is a trick to writing papers and that is to do it systematically. Don't panic and do begin early. First, you should . . .

CHOOSE YOUR SUBJECT CAREFULLY

The correct choice in most situations can be rewarding and the wrong choice can often be disastrous. This also applies in choosing your subject for a paper. If you choose a subject that is too broad or too general, you may find that there is too much material on it and you cannot possibly cover the subject adequately in one paper. For instance, a subject that would be too broad is "The Novels of Ernest Hemingway." There are literally hundreds of books about Hemingway's novels and it would be very hard for you to discuss all of them in a single paper.

If you find too much material on a broad subject, you may find too little on a narrow subject. An example might be a report on one of the minor characters in a lesser known novel by Hemingway. You could search until you were blue in the face and still not find enough for a paper if there isn't very much written on the subject.

Try not to select a subject that is over your head. There are few things more frustrating than trying to read a book or article that you cannot understand and then trying to write about it.

So choose your subject carefully, making it not too broad and not too narrow. Finally, try to select a subject that you are interested in. It's a lot easier to report on something you feel strongly about than on a subject that bores you to tears. Then . . .

MAKE A PRELIMINARY SEARCH FOR MATERIAL

First check the library catalog to see if the subject is listed. If it isn't, and if there are no related subjects, then you are in trouble. The subject is too narrow, too specialized, or too recent to be entered in the catalog. If you find the subject but there are many subtopics under it, the subject is too broad.

Now make a brief search through the periodical index that covers your subject. Again, if there are no entries or only a few articles under the entry, you may have to change the subject as you will probably need periodical articles for your paper. If the subject entry has many subtopics under it, you are out of the ball-park. Use these subtopics to get you back in. They show how the main subject is broken down into more narrow areas within this subject.

"Somehow I don't think Clark Kent had this much trouble writing his papers." (Of course not. We all know he could leap mighty libraries with a single bound!)

Suppose you want to write on the subject of ecology. There is a subject entry in the Readers' Guide under "Ecology" with several general articles discussing it. One of the clues that tells you this subject is too broad is the many "see also" references:

Birds—Ecology	Mountain ecology
Environment	Paleoecology
Food chain (ecology)	Religion and ecology
Forest ecology	Seashore ecology
Fresh water ecology	Snow ecology
Human ecology	Zoology—Ecology
Marine ecology	

All of these entries relate to the main subject entry "Ecology." Many of them may have "see also" references further narrowing the subject.

Another clue that you may have too broad a subject is the number of subtopics within the subject. For instance, in the <u>Readers' Guide</u> these are some important subtopics under the subject entry "Environment":

Conferences	Poetry
Economic aspects	Study and teaching
Laws and legislation	Terminology

Any one of these subtopics could be a subject for a paper.

Next, read an encyclopedia article. This will give you an overview. Likewise, if there is little or nothing in the encyclopedia, there may be little or nothing available in the library. A lengthy article divided into various subtopics will mean a subject too broad or general.

Let's assume that, based on your preliminary search, you have selected a subject that is adequately covered in the library catalog and periodical indexes, a subject within your range of knowledge and ability, and a subject that you would enjoy reporting on. You are now ready to start your . . .

INTRODUCTORY READING

Read a chapter in a textbook on your subject. Skim through one of the books that comprehensively covers the subject. Read one of the periodical articles. These preliminary readings will introduce you to the subject, help you further narrow it, and lead you to the next step . . .

MAKE AN OUTLINE FOR YOUR PAPER

By now you should have a handle on your subject. You have an overview from the encyclopedia and the introductory reading has given you the dimensions that you wish for limiting your paper. You should prepare a tentative outline. The outline is one of the most important elements of a paper. Can you imagine building a house without first constructing the frame? The outline is the frame of the paper and to complete the paper you need only fill in the frame. First jot down the major topics or ideas that you are going to cover.

Let's say you want to write a paper on how to construct a house. Your major topics might be:

    I.   Foundation
    II. Plumbing
    III. Frame
    IV. Ouside walls
    V.   Inside walls
    VI. Roof
    VII. Wiring
    VIII. Insulation
    IX. Finishing

From these topics you can arrive at a <u>thesis statement,</u> a statement telling the main idea of the paper. The thesis statement for this example might be, "The proper way to construct a house is to proceed in a systematic step-by-step program." This statement tells what your paper will discuss.

The outline then breaks down or divides the thesis into the topics that discuss and support it. An outline for our paper might look like this:

Thesis Statement: The proper way to construct a house is to
                   proceed in a systematic step-by-step program.
    I. Foundation (the major topic that supports the thesis)
        A. Foundation forms (a subtopic discussing the major topic
            foundation)
        B. Concrete (another subtopic under the major topic founda-
            tion)
            1. Cement
            2. Sand
            3. Water

 II. Plumbing
     A. Pipes
     B. Connecting joints
 III. Frame
 IV. Outside walls
  V. Inside walls
 VI. Roof
 VII. Wiring
 VIII. Insulation
 IX. Finishing

After you have completed the outline you should begin . . .

GATHERING YOUR SOURCE MATERIAL

Teachers like you to use the full range of information available at the library for term or research papers—the regular circulating books, periodical articles, and reference books. You already know how to locate these sources: books through the library catalog, articles through the periodical indexes, and reference books in the reference collection.

You also know that the books on the same subject will be shelved together. Use the library catalog to find the call number of one book and you have them all. Don't indiscriminately pull them off the shelf though and check them out simply because your subject is mentioned in the title. Look through the table of contents in the front of the book and the index at the back of the book to be sure the book touches exactly what you are writing about. Check the writing style to make sure the book is at the level that you need—neither so elementary that it will not be a satisfactory reference nor so scholarly that you will not understand it. With each book or periodical that you finally select as source material, you should . . .

PREPARE A BIBLIOGRAPHY CARD

A bibliography is a list of the sources that you use for writing your paper. For each book that you use, prepare a bibliography card (usually a 3" x 5" card) listing the call number, the author, title, publisher, and place and date of publication. List the page numbers that you consulted. For periodicals you should also list the identifying information. Make a bibliography card for each source you consult so that later when you prepare the bibliography you will have the information available on the cards and you won't have to go back and hunt for it.

A bibliography card might look like this:

```
TH151.V4   Ulrey, Harry F.   Building Construction
           and design.   Indianapolis, Indiana,
           Audel, 1970

           Pages 47-50
```

You are now ready to . . .

READ THE SOURCE MATERIAL AND PREPARE NOTE CARDS

As you read the source material, take notes on the facts and ideas that seem important enough for you to use in the paper. The note cards can be the 3" x 5" cards or larger. It is better to go lightly over the material first before taking any notes. This enables you to get the whole picture of the chapter or article. You can then go back and take notes on the parts that directly relate to your subject.

The notes you are taking are the building blocks that you use to complete the outline. The note cards will generally contain the following items:

1. The author and title of the book or article.
2. The topic heading from your outline to which this information applies.
3. The notes or thoughts that pertain to the topic.
4. The exact pages where the notes came from.

The outline topic heading serves to label all of the note cards that cover a particular topic. When you write the paper you can then easily assemble all the note cards under each topic.

"As I take the notes from the source material, can I use the author's exact words?"

Yes, it is permissible to use the exact wording that the author uses provided you give him credit. The way that you quote an author is to place quotation marks around the word, sentence, or phrase that he uses.

Normally when you write a term or research paper, you consult other authors' writings. It is perfectly all right to use their ideas and facts but you must express them in your own words. This does not mean simply inserting or substituting words. You must take the central idea and write it as if you were the original author, with your language and your interpretation.

When you intend to use a direct quotation, record it on the note card, making sure that you have written exactly what the original author said. Be sure to note the page where the quotation was found. Often teachers will go back and check over your sources to be sure that you have given credit to the authors and have not used their words as your own.

The usual method for crediting an author is through the use of . . .

FOOTNOTES

Footnotes are notes telling the source of a quotation. They are usually placed at the "foot" or bottom of the page on which you have written the quotation. They can also be listed on a separate page at the end of the paper.

"When should I use footnotes?"

You should use footnotes for:

1. Direct quotations, the author's exact words.
2. Figures or statistics taken from another work.
3. An original concept or opinion of an author.

"What does a footnote look like?"

The following is a footnote for this quotation: "For ventilation of attics under gabled roofs, one square foot of clear opening should be provided for each 300 square feet of ceiling area."[1]

    1. Harry F. Ulrey, <u>Building Construction and Design</u> (Indianapolis: Audel, 1970), p. 185.

Notice the number "1" after the last quotation mark at the end of the quotation. Each footnote is numbered, as you may have several for each page. This example is only one way to write footnotes; there are other ways. Ask your teacher immediately after he makes an assignment how and where he wants the footnotes. This footnote has the author's name (first name first), title of the book (underlined), the place of publication, publisher and date (in parentheses), and the page number that the quotation came from.

You may find at any time during your reading and notetaking that the outline has to be altered. You may decide to take a different course in writing the paper. Perhaps there wasn't enough material on all of the major topics.

You are moving right along though. In fact you should be ready for the . . .

FIRST DRAFT OF THE PAPER

It is always better to write a rough draft or first edition of your paper before the final product. With the outline as a guide fill in the text of the paper using your note cards for each topic as building blocks. Discuss each topic as it relates to and supports the thesis statement. Insert the footnotes where there is a need. You already know how and when to use reference books for supportive material.

Writing a rough draft accomplishes several things. You can tell approximately how long the paper is going to be.

Will you have to add or delete material, or will you have to . . .

REVISE THE ROUGH DRAFT

If you have examined the paper carefully, more than likely it will need some revision. Be sure that you have told the full story. Do the topics relate to the thesis? Have you given credit to other authors' works in the paper by using footnotes? Are the grammar and spelling correct? Are sentence and paragraph structure developed into a cohesive unit? These are but a few of the things you should check for. Finally be sure that you are fully and completely satisfied with the paper. A lot of time and effort has probably gone into writing it and a polished paper can often mean the difference between a good or a poor grade.

Believe it or not, you are ready for the . . .

FINAL COPY

If possible you should hand in a typed copy of the paper. Make it neat. Keep the margins and spacing consistent throughout the paper. Prepare a cover sheet telling the title of the paper, the author (you), the date, the course number, and the teacher.

Normally, the last page of the final copy will be the . . .

BIBLIOGRAPHY

As we previously mentioned, the bibliography is a list of the sources you have used to write your paper. It is an alphabetical listing by the author's last name. When the author is not given, the first word of the title is used in the alphabetical sequence. One way to write bibliographic entries is illustrated below. Notice the entries in a bibliography are not numbered.

Bibliography

Halperin, Don A. Building with Steel. Chicago: American Technical
    Society, 1966.
Merritt, Frederick S. Building Construction Handbook. New York:
    McGraw-Hill, 1965.
"Shelter in the Woods," Architectural Forum, March 1970, pp. 36-9.
Ulrey, Harry F. Building Construction and Design. Indianapolis:
    Audel and Co., 1970.
Wright, J.R. "Performance Criteria in Building." Scientific Ameri-
    can, March 1971, pp. 16-25.

Notice the third and fifth entries. They are periodical articles. The first is unsigned and is entered in the alphabetical listing by the first letter in the first word of the article. The second is signed and is entered alphabetically by the author's last name.

Index